MORE SHOP DRAWINGS
for
CRAFTSMAN FURNITURE

MORE
SHOP DRAWINGS
for
CRAFTSMAN
FURNITURE

30 Stickley Designs for Every Room in the Home

Measured and drawn by
ROBERT W. LANG

CAMBIUM PRESS

Bethel, CT

MORE Shop Drawings For Craftsman Furniture
30 Stickley Designs for Every Room in the Home

ISBN 1-892836-14-9
First printing: October 2002
Second printing: March 2004
Published by
    Cambium Press
    PO Box 909
    Bethel, CT 06801
      203-778-5610
      www.CAMBIUMPRESS.com

Library of Congress Cataloging-in-Publication Data

Lang, Robert W. 1953-
    More shop drawings for Craftsman furniture: 30 Stickley designs for every room in the home
    /measured and drawn by Robert W. Lang.
    p. cm.
    Includes index.
    ISBN 1-892836-14-9 (alk. paper.)
    1. Furniture--Drawings. 2. Measured drawings. 3. Arts and crafts movement. I. Title.
    TT196 .L3497 2002
    684.1'04--dc21
                2002151911

DEDICATION

I would like to thank my wife Joyce and my son Hunter for their patience, love, and support during this work. They are the ones who did the hard work, and I am truly grateful to them as well as for them.

CONTENTS

DINING ROOM   page 26

No. 552
Gate Leg Table 28

No. 624
Hexagonal Table 32

No. 353 Side Chair
No. 353A Arm Chair
36

No. 800
Sideboard
40

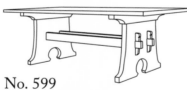

No. 599
Large Trestle Table 45

No. 719
Glass Corner
Cabinet
48

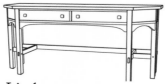

Limbert
Console Table 53

No. 962
Serving Table 56

No.729
China Cabinet
60

No. 803
Harvey Ellis
China Cabinet
64

No. 66
Wall Mirror
68

LIVING ROOM page 71

No. 336
Bow-Arm
Morris
Chair 72

No. 347
Eastwood Easy
Chair 80

No. 206
Love
Seat
Settle
88

No. 323
Rocker 76

No. 1292
Footstool 85

No.225
Small Settle 92

BEDROOM page 97

No. 911
Dresser
with Mirror
98

Gustav Stickley
Queen-Size Bed 103

No. 110
Nightstand
113

Limbert
Vanity Table
with Mirror
108

LIBRARY & DEN page 117

No. 74
Bookrack with
Keyed Tenons
118

No. 72
Harvey Ellis
Magazine Stand
123

No. 503
Desk with
Bookcase
Ends 134

No. 644
Open
Bookcase
120

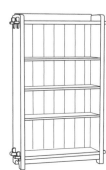

No. 724
Drop-Front
Ladies Desk 126

No.637
Library
Table 131

No. 616
Library Table w.
2 Drawers 138

Limbert
Lamp Table 141

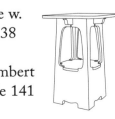

INTRODUCTION

Two years ago, on a perfect Indian-summer afternoon, Publisher John Kelsey and I met to decide which pieces of furniture to include in my first book, *Shop Drawings for Craftsman Furniture*. We had spent the morning at an auction of genuine Craftsman pieces, and had enjoyed lunch at the Hancock Shaker Village in western Massachusetts. It was a fitting place for us to meet, for it was here that Ejner Handberg had measured the furniture for his books of drawings of Shaker furniture. Handberg's work had a tremendous influence on me as a beginning woodworker, and the thought that somebody should do a similar book on Craftsman furniture led me to create my first book.

It became immediately apparent that the task was not to decide what pieces to include, but what pieces to leave out. I had been through the reproduction catalogs and other sources, picking what I thought were good examples of the style. I arrived with a list of more than two hundred pieces that I thought worthy of inclusion. Kelsey had his own favorites, and there were some pieces at the auction that neither of us had seen before. From this collection of about two hundred and fifty excellent examples of furniture, we figured that about sixty pieces would make a good book. We decided to group the furniture in categories: bedroom, dining room, living room, library or den.

By the end of the afternoon, we had the list down to around one hundred pieces of furniture, and I made the final cut to sixty something over the next few weeks. It was difficult. The final choices were based on what I personally liked, and when I couldn't make a decision, on what my wife liked.

A project like this can't be exhaustive. My aim was to show enough examples of enough different types of furniture for the reader to get a good grasp of this style of furniture, and to be able to apply the construction techniques to other projects, be they reproductions, adaptations, or entirely new designs.

As I worked on the drawings and the text for the first book, we soon realized that there was simply more good material than one book could hold. We decided to divide the material into two volumes.

This doesn't mean that the pieces of furniture included in this volume are also-rans to the pieces in the first book. The process of choosing sixty good examples was difficult enough, but splitting that group in half was even harder. In many cases, the flip of a coin decided which piece went first. In the end, I think that this grouping is equal to or better than the one in the original book. I invited visitors to my website to suggest pieces that they would like to see included in this or future works, and nearly all of the suggestions I received were already on my list.

The text portion in this book is also a continuation of the first book, along with some material included as a result of questions that we have received. The reader who by chance has picked up this book first needs to know that there is some important material in the first volume, which does not reappear here. The first book includes a detailed explanation of how to interpret and work with these drawings, techniques for making common joints, and an introduction to materials. This book focuses on assembly techniques, joinery techniques, and upholstery.

The legacy of Gustav Stickley provides us with much more than the opportunity to reproduce excellent examples of furniture design. As I have studied his work and writings, I have also found a wonderful example of the profound importance of the way that we perform our daily work, and the importance of working with something genuine, something that will carry the effort we put

into it well beyond our passing. It is my hope that the current interest in this furniture will spark a renewed interest in the philosophy and moral values that led to its original creation. In much the same way that Craftsman furniture can fill a need in our homes, the Craftsman philosophy can also fill a need in our lives.

ABOUT THE DRAWINGS

A few reminders about the drawings are in order. First of all, we have given all measurements in inches and fractions to the nearest sixteenth, followed [in square brackets] by the exact metric equivalent, down to tenths of a millimeter. This allows the metric worker to do his own rounding up or down, to the degree of precision he finds most comfortable. Dimensions in the drawings are for overall sizes, openings, and exposed areas. For doors and drawers, the numbers give the size of the finished opening, and the builder must decide the actual size of the door or drawer front. For panels, the numbers show the distance exposed between the stiles and rails, so the actual panel will be slightly larger, and the overall lengths must be longer to accommodate the joints. In the material lists that accompany the drawings, there are notes reflecting this. Also, in the material lists, pieces with tenons will be listed with an overall size, plus an "exposed" or "between tenons" dimension.

I try to include dimensions for parts only once, in the view where they make the most sense; for example, length in elevations, width and depth in plans, etc. If it seems that a necessary dimension is missing, study all of the views. In some cases you will have to add, subtract, or divide the given dimensions to find the size of an individual part. Time invested in studying the drawings before beginning construction will be well rewarded once you start to build.

Making the Quadralinear Leg

As attractive as the face of quartersawn white oak can be, the edge grain tends to be downright ugly, particularly when seen next to a beautifully flecked surface. On table tops or case tops, the edge generally doesn't have enough surface area for this difference in appearance to be a real aesthetic problem. Square legs, however, are another story. The leg looks funny if the quartersawn rays do not appear on adjacent surfaces, even though it isn't possible to have rays on both the face and the edge of a single board.

Gustav Stickley recognized this, and his solution was simply to laminate two (or more) pieces of quartersawn stock together, then to veneer over the two side surfaces. There are two ways in which this seemingly reasonable solution can cause problems. The first problem is in finishing — if the work is to be stained or dyed, the veneer and the solid wood will each take the stain differently, and there's liable to be a difference in color or shade between the two surfaces. This is not insurmountable, but it will require some extra effort to match the coloring on both types of surfaces. The same problem will also occur when fuming — the tannic acid content of the solid wood and of the veneer will be different, unless the veneers were cut from the same pieces of wood used for the solid parts. Again, this is not the end of the world, but some amount of toning or shading will likely be necessary.

The second problem, which is more troublesome, is that of wood movement between the solid material and the veneer. Unlike plain-sawn wood, the quartered pieces will expand and contract more in thickness than in width. This movement won't match the seasonal movement of the veneer, and it is quite likely that the veneer eventually will crack. The majority of original Gustav Stickley pieces that I have seen exhibit this cracking. Usually it is rather minor, occurring for an inch or two near the bottom of the leg, and I can't honestly say how long it may take for this cracking to develop, or if it will occur at all. It is troubling, however, to see such a flaw in an otherwise perfect piece of furniture, even if it is close to one hundred years old. A thicker veneer, sawn from the same wood that is used for the other parts of the leg, might reduce the chances of cracking, and might be a better match for color and figure. There are now veneers available with backings applied to them, either a second layer of cross-grain veneer, or of paper, or of paper impregnated with phenolic resin. These also may reduce the problem of cracking, but will introduce their own problems of matching the figure and color in finishing.

Leopold Stickley came up with a solution that was both elegant in appearance, and eminently practical for production in a factory setting. Figure 1 shows his method of

Quartersawn or rift sawn

Most shrinkage in this direction

Most shrinkage in this direction

Plainsawn

"Quadralinear" construction, and one of the pieces. Four pieces of solid quarter-sawn wood are joined with a rabbeted miter. This method eliminates the two problems mentioned previously. The leg is all solid construction, the core can be filled with another piece of wood if there has to be an exposed tenon, and with the machinery available then, as well as today, it is relatively simple to produce.

The same visual effect could be achieved if the pieces were simply mitered, but with Leopold's ingenious system, the joints can be clamped together without the tendency to slide apart that simple miters would have. Also, all four pieces are machined identically — there are no rights or lefts or fronts or backs to keep track of, so the set up work for milling needs to be done only one time for any number of legs.

My guess is that these legs were originally milled in the factory in one pass on a shaper or molder, a machine that was in use in factories of the period, but is unfortunately not affordable for the average woodworker of today. This joint can easily be cut on a tablesaw, and there are several alternative ways to make a joint that is just as easily assembled, with the same finished appearance. The key to success in any of these methods lies in careful stock preparation, and being absolutely sure that the position of the stock does not change as the wood moves past the cutter. Due to the nature of this joint, any error will result in a gap twice as large as the deviation. For example, if you try to make a long miter cut on a board with a bow of 1/32" over its length, the end result will be a 1/16" gap in the finished joint. Similarly, if the board should raise up slightly while moving past the sawblade, a gap of twice that distance will result. Careful set-up, featherboards, hold-downs, or a power feeder will go a long way toward ensuring the successful milling of this joint.

Figures 2, 3, & 4 show the sequence of cuts to make this joint with a tablesaw. First, two grooves are milled in the back face of the board. Note that these grooves are offset; the exact distance will depend on the thickness and width of the wood. The groove that is closest to the edge could be the width of the saw blade, but I generally cut it with the dado head since that will be in the saw for cutting the other groove. Next, a miter is cut from one outside corner to the bottom corner of this groove. Lastly, the opposite edge is mitered, leaving a flat-bottomed rabbet. Take great care when cutting this last miter, since the flat surface that is left to bear against the saw table is rather small. If a feather board is used, locate it away from the fence so that it bears on the flat of the workpiece. Use a push stick, which should also bear on the middle of the board. Pressure on the board close to the saw fence will cause that edge of the board to

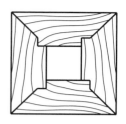

1.

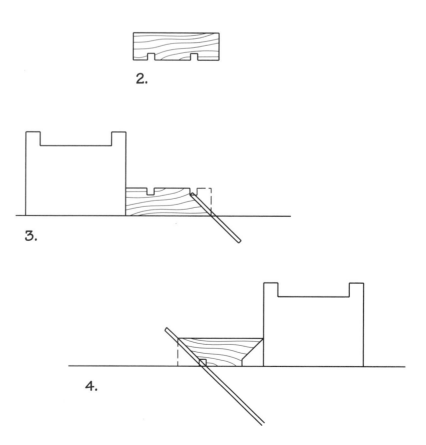

2.

3.

4.

5.

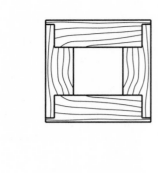

6.

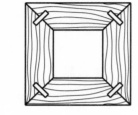

7.

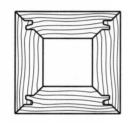

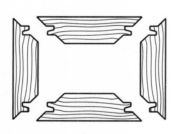

tip down, ruining the cut.

These illustrations are drawn assuming a left-tilt table saw, and are shown from the infeed side of the saw. If using a right-tilt saw, the fence positions and angle of the blade will be opposite of that shown. These cuts could also be made on a shaper or a router table.

Some alternative methods are shown in the following illustrations, and it should be remembered that simple miters could do the job. The biggest drawback to simple miters is that they tend to slide while being clamped during assembly. One method I have used successfully to glue together long miters is to place all four pieces face up on the bench, with their long edges touching. Apply clear packing tape along the length of each joint. Once the tape is applied, flip the assembly over, add glue, the pieces can be folded together, and the final joint taped together. This works well if the parts are carefully cut, and with modern glues the joint will be more than strong enough.

Figure 5 shows a stepped rabbet joint. This method avoids the cutting of miters, but it should be noted that the glue line will be offset from the corner, and not directly on the corner as in the mitered joints. If the edges are slightly rounded or beveled, the glue line will disappear where the edge of the bevel meets the face of the leg.

Figure 6 shows a miter joint reinforced with splines running the length of each joint. Biscuits could also be used. The advantage of splines or biscuits is to keep the parts aligned while also adding some strength.

Figure 7 shows a lock miter joint. Available as a router bit or a shaper cutter, this joint is a good alternative to the authentic joint, and is probably the most efficient alternative, particularly if a shaper with a power feeder is available. Setting up this joint may take some time, but once done, a sample can be kept for future set-ups. The pieces should be rough-cut over-size to 45 degrees so the router or shaper is only milling the joint, not removing the entire edge of the board.

Once assembled, the leg can be treated as a single piece of wood, although it would be prudent to insert a carefully sized core piece wherever joints will occur. Whatever method is used, acceptable results will come only if all the pieces to be milled are truly straight, flat, and square, and they are kept flat to the saw table, and tight against the saw fence.

JOINERY DETAILS

The only photograph I have seen of the inside of Gustav Stickley's Craftsman Workshops shows joiners at work, some nearly completed bookcases, and a desk. The floor is nearly covered with plane shavings, and light streams into the room from a row of windows above the workbenches. It would be easy to imagine that these men had made the furniture entirely by hand, from start to finish. Stickley's factory was, however, quite modern for the period, and was equipped with early versions of most of the machinery commonly seen in furniture factories of today. The men in the picture assembled and fitted pieces from parts that came to them cut to size, likely with the mortises and tenons already machined. Their job was to assemble the pieces, fine-tuning the fit and finish of the joints, the doors and drawers, and drawer fronts.

One of the difficulties of production furniture-making is that no matter how carefully and accurately parts are cut, wood will move slightly from day to day, and parts that fit perfectly yesterday might not go easily together today. Wood just doesn't cooperate with precision machining techniques, and it takes a keen eye and a practiced hand to produce truly excellent work. A little adjustment here and there is almost always necessary, both in a home workshop and in furniture factories. The joiners in Stickley's factory had the luxury of practicing the most skilled and most demanding parts of their trade without the heavy, unskilled labor.

Gustav Stickley was not against the use of machinery, in fact he saw it as a way to relieve the worker of drudgery. His written objections to machine-made furniture were mostly aimed at issues of style and quality — furniture that pretended to be something it was not, with useless ornamentation covering up shoddy work. At the turn of the

Twentieth Century, the attitude of most woodworkers toward powered saws, joiners, planers and shapers was likely one of welcome relief. Gustav Stickley's production methods used the skills of his workers for the details that needed the human touch, and efficiently used available machinery wherever it was appropriate.

We tend to romanticize handwork without looking at the reality of what is involved in doing it. In my own work, I try to judge what is the most appropriate, most efficient method. Sometimes it is a hand tool or hand technique, and sometimes it is a machine. I don't find any pleasure in working harder than necessary for the sake of authenticity, if the results come out the same. Nearly every project in *Mission Furniture — How to Make It* (originally published as articles in *Popular Mechanics* magazine during the period) begins with the advice to have someone with machinery cut and plane the wood.

Stickley designed his furniture for production in a factory setting, and many of the changes that occurred from one year's production to the next reflect ways of producing the pieces more efficiently, or less expensively. The details left to be done by hand reflect a wise use of available resources, both machine, and human. Efficiency in production makes equal sense to the owner of a factory, a small modern shop with one or two furniture-makers trying to earn a living, and to the hobbyist trying to make something for his own enjoyment in his scarce leisure time.

In *Shop Drawings for Craftsman Furniture*, I covered most of the joining methods used originally, and offered my preferences along with some other alternatives. I don't want to repeat myself, but a few of the fine points and little details were not covered in as much detail as I would have liked.

Many of these fine details aren't really possible to show in mechanical drawings. Their

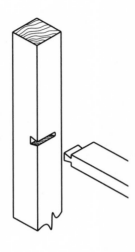

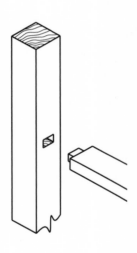

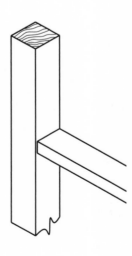

Rail to leg joints.

execution provides evidence of different sets of hands on the originals, as well as an opportunity for today's woodworker to develop his own skills and style. Edges and corners are generally given a very slight chamfer, what I would call a broken edge. The chamfer is not large enough to call attention to itself, but it's no longer a sharp corner either. There is considerable variation in both the size and the shape of this edge-treatment in the original examples. Sometimes the edges have more of a radius than a chamfer, and the size of the chamfer or radius can vary from nearly nothing to an eighth of an inch.

These variations occur both in types of pieces — chairs tend to have more of a radiused edge than casework and tables -- and also between two examples of the same piece. These differences could be the result of wear over time, but I think that different departments in the factory, and different individuals, had their own distinct way of doing things. Some workers prefer a tiny crisp chamfer cut with a stroke or two of a plane, while others prefer a softer and more rounded edge developed by lightly sanding the corner. Neither one is right or wrong — choose the method or look that works for you.

Exposed tenons and especially keyed tenons exhibit more evidence of handwork, and more variations in the execution of these details. Generally, there will be more of a chamfer or radius on these exposed joints than on the rest of the piece, and again, these are sometimes seen chamfered, and sometimes rounded. In the drawings I show these larger details as I found them on the individual piece I studied. There will likely be another

example of the same piece, done a little differently. The worker building a reproduction is once again left to make a decision based on his or her own preferences.

Drawer and door fronts are set back slightly — no more than one-sixteenth of an inch — from adjacent frames. Horizontal rails are often set back by a similar amount from vertical stiles or legs. I have shown these setbacks in the drawings, and have included dimensions where space permits. Where dimensions are not given, the reader can safely assume that the setback is slight.

Another place where details are often not shown precisely is in small joints, such as front rails on case pieces, and the joints between elements in glass doors or case sides. Rails were originally mortised and tenoned, but the reproductions currently manufactured by L. & J.G. Stickley use a hidden dovetail joint, an idea said to have been developed by Leopold Stickley in the 1920s when the factory switched to reproductions of early American furniture. There is no difference in appearance in the finished piece, but I think the hidden dovetail is a great improvement, both from a structural standpoint and for ease in assembly. Driven into their half-blind sockets from behind, these joints will hold the cabinet sides together mechanically. The key element in making these joints is to maintain the correct distance between the two shoulders of the dovetailed ends. The sockets can be made either on a router table or with a hand held router. Adjustments in fit should be made on the tails at the ends of the rails, and the tails will need a relief cut to bring the fronts flush, so that from the front it appears to be a butt joint. The dovetails could be through and exposed on the front if you want to show them off, but this detail would not be authentic.

DUST PANELS

Some people are surprised by the absence of dust panels in between drawers in case pieces such as dressers. This is generally the way this furniture was originally manufactured. Dust panels can be added by building a frame behind the front rail, and adding a thin panel inside the frame. This will impart some strength to the case, though in most pieces it will be overbuilding a structure that is already very sturdy.

One design element that could use improvement is the absence of a rail above the top drawer in case pieces. Gustav Stickley liked to have the top of the drawer directly under the case top, and his many imitators followed his lead. Visually it is an important element in his furniture, but in many original examples that I have seen, the unsupported top sags over time, either dragging at the center of the drawer or pulling loose where it is supported at the sides of the case. This condition can be improved by adding a hidden rail behind the top of the drawer front. This will provide both a means of support and a way to attach the top to the case, and the only real impact is to reduce the height of the drawer by the thickness of the rail.

GLASS DOORS

Muntins and mullions on glass doors or case sides should be mortised and tenoned to the adjacent stiles and rails, and either mortises and tenons or half lap joints are appropriate at their intersections. Most of these pieces are small, and with a rabbet on the back to accommodate the glass, there is not much room left for a tenon. I line up the edges of the mortises with the edges of the rabbets as shown in the drawing at left. Some early examples had mitered joints at these points, but this method of production

did not remain in use for long. It does make for an attractive glass door, but it is more demanding to construct and I think it is not as strong as it ought to be; these are probably why these were changed.

Original examples of Craftsman furniture demonstrate good, sound construction techniques. I have raised a few minor points regarding things that I have seen fail in original examples, but it should be remembered that these are minor, usually cosmetic flaws in furniture that is nearly one hundred years old. On the whole, this furniture teaches us a wonderful lesson in technique, as well in as design and proportion.

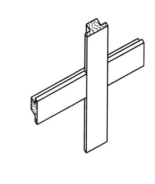

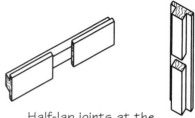

Half-lap joints at the middle of glass doors.

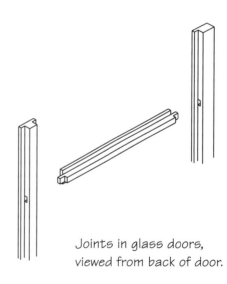

Joints in glass doors, viewed from back of door.

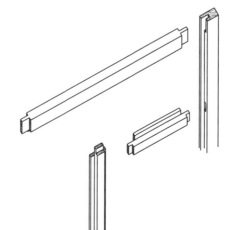

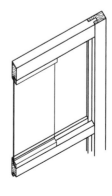

LAYING OUT & MAKING PATTERNS

One of the traditional ways of taking the step from drawing to building is the story pole, essentially a full size representation of important details from the drawing. This is an excellent way to work out joinery details, and to transfer measurements from one part to another without repetitiously measuring. The exact form of the story pole will vary depending on the size and complexity of the piece to be built. A stick of wood, 3/4" x 1-3/4" is commonly used, but in some cases, a wider piece may be more appropriate, up to a piece the actual size of a finished part. I tend to use 3/4" thick Melamine covered particleboard because lines drawn on it are easy to see, pencil lines can be erased with a damp rag, and I usually have some around. If I had to buy a 4' x 8' sheet to use only for story poles, I would probably switch to the traditional stick of hardwood.

I usually make three separate story poles, one for height, one for width, and one for depth. The stick representing height may show details for the front of the piece on one surface, and details for the side on the adjacent surface. For complicated cases, there may be two distinct sticks, one representing drawer or door locations on the front of the finished case, and the other showing details of the paneled sides. Often it is helpful to draw a full-size plan view or a section on a piece of light-colored plywood or Melamine board to aid in visualizing the work, and to check things as the work progresses.

Story poles are cut to the exact length of the finished piece of furniture, so the locations of intersecting pieces and joints can be marked out full size. Take your time, and work carefully and precisely. I write notes on the stick, and mark with an X areas that will be removed. When parts have been cut to size,

say four legs for a dresser or desk, the parts will be clamped together, and the locations for intersections and joints transferred from the story pole with a square. This saves a good deal of time and reduces the possibility of a mathematical or measurement error. If the piece is ever to be made again in the future, all of the layout work is already complete, saving a step in the production process.

As the work progresses, story poles can be used to check subassemblies and parts to be sure that the plan is being followed, and that the work is as it should be. Changes and corrections can also be noted directly on the pole for future reference.

CURVED PARTS

For chair legs, or other parts that are curved, it is a good idea to go a step further, and make a full-size pattern of the part. This is particularly helpful when making chairs, since these are usually made in multiples, and the layout can be complicated and time-consuming. The pattern for chair legs can also incorporate templates for routing mortises, so that in use the chair leg can be cut slightly oversize, attached to the pattern, and then trimmed to finish size with a router and a flush-cutting bit. A second router with a guide collar can then cut the mortises for the joints. If using this method, remember to size the mortise openings in the pattern according to the guide collar. I usually write the collar and bit combination right on the pattern, to avoid confusion later.

Arched aprons or rails can be laid out with a beam compass or trammel points set to the radius given in the drawings, and this is another time when a full-size pattern can be useful, particularly if the piece contains more than one arched element, or if it is likely that this piece will be made again. These radii can be awkwardly long, and it can be difficult to accurately locate the center of the arc if it is very far from the edge of the workpiece. The arc can be laid out by locating its midpoint and its two ends, driving in brads at these points, and bending a thin strip of wood around them. Any tenons or other joints on the ends of arc-shaped pieces are easier to make first, before sawing the arc itself.

Usually the bottom of the arc starts about half-an-inch in from the end of the apron, and the intersection of the arc and the short straight section is radiused slightly after cutting the arc. This is to keep the end of the apron at a defined size. If the arc went right to the end of the part, it would terminate in a point, and sanding or otherwise smoothing the inside of the curve would reduce the height of the part at that point.

Some curved pieces shown in the drawings include a 1" square grid as a layout aid. By re-creating the grid full size, you can locate the intersections of the curved line and the grid, and develop a full-size pattern of the part. Once these points are located, a thin strip of wood can be bent across the points, and the curve drawn by running a pencil along the edge of the curved strip.

RIGHTS AND LEFTS

Most of the pieces in this book have parts that will only go in one place, for example, a dresser or other case piece will have four legs that are identical in size and shape, but the joints cut in each will be on opposing sides depending on the orientation of the piece. These should be marked in some way so that you don't end up with two left front legs, and no right front legs. I mark legs on the bottom or top with simple designations in pencil, indicating not only which piece is which, but also which face of the part is the front. In general, the nicest face should be on the front of the furniture. After the joints are laid out and cut, it should be obvious which piece is which.

Triangles can be drawn across several pieces of a subassembly, or a group such as four legs, in order to maintain their orientation. I was taught that the triangle's point always faces up, or always faces to the right. I also add a line parallel to one or more of the legs of the triangle if there are more than one identical assemblies. I usually draw these with chalk so that I don't have to worry about removing pencil lines later on.

TENON JIG

If nothing else, making Craftsman style furniture will provide an opportunity to practice woodworking joints, and in some pieces, an opportunity to practice, practice, practice making joints. For mortises, I prefer the hollow chisel mortiser. A good plunge router, with the right bits and jigs, is nearly as fast but for me, it is too noisy, dusty, and hard to hang on to for any extended period of time. For tenons, my preference is for a jig on the tablesaw. The example shown here is made from 3/4"-thick Baltic birch plywood, with a replaceable hardwood fence, and an adjustable hold-down clamp.

When it comes time to fit the joints, I find it easier to fit the tenon to the mortise. With this jig, the saw can be set accurately in the first place, then adjusted to remove a small fraction of the tenon, with the tablesaw's fence mechanism utilized for making fine, precise adjustments.

Construction of this jig is simple, it is basically the shape of a small letter h with the inside of the bottom of the h sized to fit over the fence of the saw. The width of the horizontal piece is the only critical dimension in the whole jig, because it must be sized so that the jig will fit over the saw fence and slide freely, but not so tight that it will bind.

The height of the short piece should be close to the height of the fence, but it is better if it

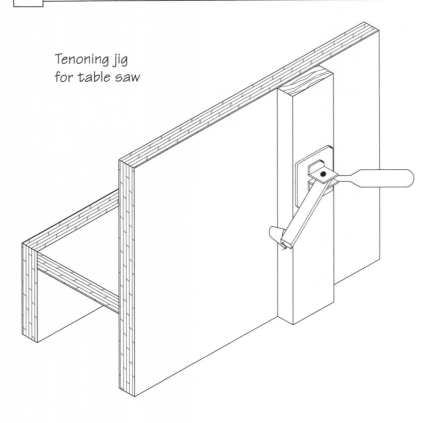

Tenoning jig
for table saw

down. I mark the depth of the cut (height of the blade) directly on the workpiece, and clamp it in the jig. Placing the jig over the saw fence, the fence is then slid toward the blade. The blade is then raised, and the height can be judged by the line on the workpiece. The distance from the fence to the blade can also be set to lines drawn on the workpiece. I make the initial setting a little wider than it should be, and then use the scale on the saw fence to get the exact size. This is a good way to fine-tune the cut, since an error on the first attempt won't ruin the workpiece. I usually make the cut on the side away from the fence, but since I am only cutting the cheek, this doesn't really matter.

After the cheeks have been cut, I make the shoulder cuts either on the tablesaw with the miter gauge, or on a sliding compound miter saw with the blade set to the proper height above the saw table. The shoulder cuts can be made slightly deeper than necessary, so that if the cheeks need to be trimmed later on, the step of cutting the cheeks does not need to be repeated. If in fitting the tenon to its mortise the tenon is too large, the piece can be returned to the jig, and the fence adjusted, remembering to take an equal amount off both sides.

Usually a combination sawblade works well for this operation, but in the case of an extremely long tenon, it can be helpful to switch to a ripping blade, as this is actually the type of cut that is being made.

Before turning on the saw, and adjusting the fence and blade for the actual cut, be sure the jig slides freely along the fence, and the workpiece is securely clamped to the jig. Make sure the blade insert for the saw is perfectly flush to the tabletop, so that the work piece or the jig does not catch on the insert.

does not touch the top of the fence at all. This way, the bottoms and insides of the two vertical pieces are the only points of friction, and they can be sanded smooth and waxed.

The other dimensions of the jig are not critical. A width of 8" and a height of 12" are good starting points for the tall upright piece, but these can be adapted depending on the work at hand. A handle in the center of the horizontal piece provides a way to push the jig past the sawblade. The fence is solid wood, and should be thick enough to back up the cut to reduce tear-out, and wide enough to allow for secure fastening of the hold-down clamp. It should be held to the tall vertical piece with screws only, as it will need to be replaced periodically. It can be attached at an angle to make the cuts on angled tenons. For safety, attach a tailpiece to the jig to cover the sawblade as you push the jig over the saw table.

In setting up to use the jig, the height of the blade is set first, before the fence is locked

Once all the adjustments have been made, clamp the work to the jig, and with the right hand on the handle over the fence, push past the blade to make the cut. I carefully slide the jig back past the blade so that I am removing and turning the workpiece at the infeed side of the saw. I feel that this is safer than trying to remove or unload the jig on the outfeed side, or reaching over the blade to adjust the workpiece.

ASSEMBLY

Building a piece of furniture with many intricate parts can be intimidating, but putting together a box is simple. When planning what steps to take to put a piece of furniture together, I try to look for the box, that is, to look at the piece as subassemblies rather than as many individual parts. A chair or a case piece can usually be seen as having two sides, plus a front and a back. Sides usually can be put together as units, so that final assembly is greatly simplified. In the drawings that contain exploded views, I have tried to show subassemblies as I would put them together. My inclination is to put sides together first, although with chairs it may be preferable to assemble the front and back first. Once the glue has thoroughly dried, these subassemblies can be treated as single pieces during the next stage of assembly.

I generally use yellow glue, which doesn't have a very long open time. If a piece is particularly complicated, I use a slow drying formula so that I don't have to rush.

When putting furniture together, I try to have as many of the parts as I possibly can nearly ready to be finished before final assembly. I sand parts to the next to the finest grit, so that once the piece is put together, the intersections of adjoining parts are the only places where there might be some work to be done, and a final hand-sanding is the only sanding left. It is much easier to completely sand individual parts, and sanding before assembly reduces the risk of introducing cross-grain scratches.

If the joints are worked carefully and accurately, then any work beyond the final glue up will be kept to a minimum. If the back of a piece can be added as the very last step, it will make finishing of the entire piece significantly easier, since the inside can be reached from the front or back, and there will be fewer inside corners to deal with.

When the time comes to do the final assembly, I begin with a dry run to be sure that all of the joints fit properly, and that I have all of the clamps, pads, and anything else I may need close at hand and ready for the final glue-up. The best way to ensure that the final assembly goes well is to be very careful when making parts, and in putting together of subassemblies. Sizes of parts should be double-checked, and joints should be test-fit. Panels and other subassemblies need to be put together square and without any twists or bows from improper clamping. If these early steps are done well, then problems at the end will be minimized.

Two elements of assembling furniture that are often overlooked are the necessity of having a flat and level surface on which to do the final assembly, and the need to have a way of holding the work square during assembly. Right-angle clamps hold corners together quite nicely and I usually apply them to hold the parts in alignment while clamping or fastening. In many shops the tablesaw is the only decent flat surface, and if you are not too sloppy with the glue, it makes a good work surface for this all-important stage of furniture-making.

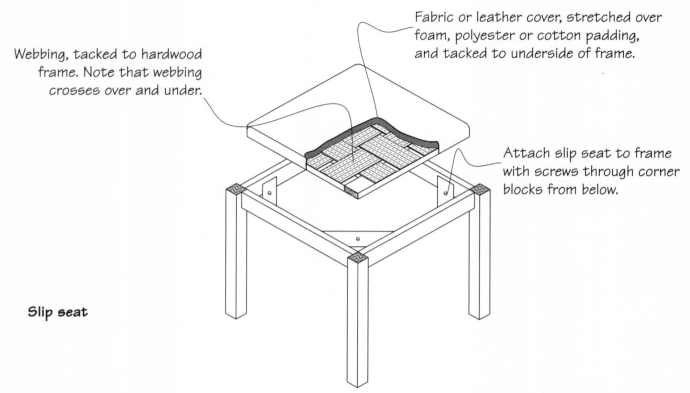

Webbing, tacked to hardwood frame. Note that webbing crosses over and under.

Fabric or leather cover, stretched over foam, polyester or cotton padding, and tacked to underside of frame.

Attach slip seat to frame with screws through corner blocks from below.

Slip seat

UPHOLSTERY

In the drawings in this book, as in the first volume *Shop Drawings for Craftsman Furniture*, upholstered seats are shown without much detail. While this could be attributed to laziness on my part, there are actually some good reasons for this fuzziness. The original pieces of furniture used several different types of cushions — some of them appear to be changes in manufacturing methods over time, while others likely were optional ways of ordering the furniture. Also, the seat cushions are the least durable part of old chairs and settles, so original examples are often seen either with the cushions missing entirely, or with some sort of replacement cushion. If you are making chairs or settles, you will need to make your own decision based on your own desire for comfort, and your skills and budget.

Upholstering is a distinct trade from woodworking, and I will confess that I am far from an expert. Slip seats on dining chairs are relatively simple to produce, and are not very demanding. Large cushions on settles and Morris chairs, with their necessary supporting structure, are more involved, and I think the best advice for the do-it-yourselfer is to either take a class on techniques, or hire someone competent to perform this work. I will review the basic methods and materials, and leave a more detailed description of how to do it to those more experienced than me. Van Dyke's Restorers (800-558-1234, www.vandykes.com) is a good source both for supplies, and for reference material. Local community colleges and vocational schools often offer classes in upholstery, and this would be a good way to learn the fine points, and to get access to needed tools and machinery capable of sewing leather and other upholstery fabrics.

The simplest cushions are found in dining chairs. Usually these were a slip seat -- leather wrapped around a padded wooden frame, attached to the frame of the chair itself by screws from below, usually through corner blocks. Occasionally the frame and padding was attached to the chair before the fabric, and the leather was fastened to the outside of the chair frame with decorative tacks. Morris chairs, large easy chairs, and settles had a greater variety of cushions, and exhibit more changes over time with new technologies and production methods.

Slip seats are simple to make. A hardwood frame, of pieces 3/4" x 1-3/4" to 2", is made to fit inside the frame of the chair itself, with an allowance around the edges for the fabric. A piece of plywood could be used, but the open area in the inside of the hardwood frame will allow air to circulate through the padding and fabric. It also looks nicer if anyone ever peeks under your chair.

If you use an open frame, place some webbing across the opening to keep the padding from falling through, and to provide some support in the middle of the seat. Padding comes next, and depending on the choice of materials, it can be either glued or tacked in place. It is easiest to wrap the fabric around the seat if it is placed good side down on a clean bench or table. Place the padded seat on top of the fabric, wrap the edges of the fabric around the edges of the frame, and tack or staple it down. Working opposite edges will make it easier to pull the fabric evenly, and to get it tight without distortion. Where the fabric meets at the corners on the underside, it is best to fold it so that adjacent edges meet at a mitered edge. After tacking down both sides, the excess fabric can be trimmed so that there is no bump at the corners. If you use your wife's good scissors, put them back before she finds out that you borrowed them. The completed seat can then be attached to the chair frame, and this is generally done by screwing from below through corner blocks or cleats.

The earliest versions of Gustav Stickley's larger chairs and settles used a woven cane support attached inside the frame of the chair, with a loose cushion on top of that. Some chairs had a canvas or leather sling, secured to the chair frame at the inside front and back. Both the cane and the sling supports have a bit of give to them, resulting in more comfort than the slip seat provides. Unfortunately, neither cane nor slings last forever, and chairs made this way are most likely to be missing their original supports. Later versions of chairs and settles had eight-way tied coil springs, either in a wooden frame that attached to the chair frame, or directly attached to the chair frame. One of Leopold Stickley's innovations was the drop-in spring unit, an idea apparently borrowed from the fledgling automobile industry. This was a metal frame containing springs, wrapped and upholstered, and dropped-in the finished chair frame.

An upholstered seat functions much like the suspension system of a car, and high quality seating comes from a balanced combination of both spring support and cushion materials. The main function of cushions is to provide comfort by compressing under load, and by keeping the body separated from a hard surface. The main function of springs is to provide support, yet be flexible enough so that when weight is shifted the point of support also shifts, and the cushion is not forced to take the entire load.

For maximum comfort, and for long life of the cushions, springs are a necessity, either coil springs supported by webbing, or the more modern sinuous wire springs (also known as "no-sag").

Cushions can be supported either by a piece of plywood or by wooden slats, and this method is often used by antique dealers to replace missing upholstery. Cotton filled futon cushions can be ordered to size at nearly any store that sells futon mattresses. Slats are preferred to plywood, because the spaces between slats will allow air to circulate

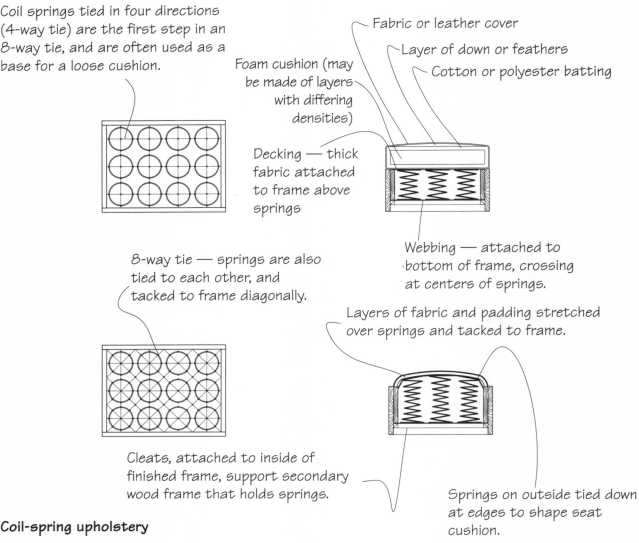

Coil springs tied in four directions (4-way tie) are the first step in an 8-way tie, and are often used as a base for a loose cushion.

Foam cushion (may be made of layers with differing densities)

Fabric or leather cover

Layer of down or feathers

Cotton or polyester batting

Decking — thick fabric attached to frame above springs

Webbing — attached to bottom of frame, crossing at centers of springs.

8-way tie — springs are also tied to each other, and tacked to frame diagonally.

Layers of fabric and padding stretched over springs and tacked to frame.

Cleats, attached to inside of finished frame, support secondary wood frame that holds springs.

Springs on outside tied down at edges to shape seat cushion.

Coil-spring upholstery

through the cushion. This is the least expensive, simplest-to-construct option, but it is also the least comfortable, and shortest lived. The problem with this method is that the chair or settle will feel stiff, and the futon or other cushion material, taking the full load of the sitter, will become compressed. As time goes on the seat will get harder and harder. This can be minimized by regularly turning the cushions. Wear on the fabric covering will also be greater with this method than with springs.

Sinuous wire springs are a step above slats and a cushion. These zigzag shaped springs are easily attached either to the chair frame, or to a separate frame, and are usually cov-

ered with a stiff fabric. The cushion then rests on top. While they provide decent support, they are not as comfortable nor as long lasting as coil springs. They are a relatively inexpensive option, and function best in smaller seats.

Properly tied and supported coil springs are the most expensive choice, as well as the most comfortable and longest lasting method for supporting seating. Jute webbing is attached in a crisscross pattern and a coil spring is attached with staples at each intersection of the webbing. Each spring is then tied with heavy twine either to the frame or to adjacent springs. A stiff fabric decking may be applied, as with the sinuous springs,

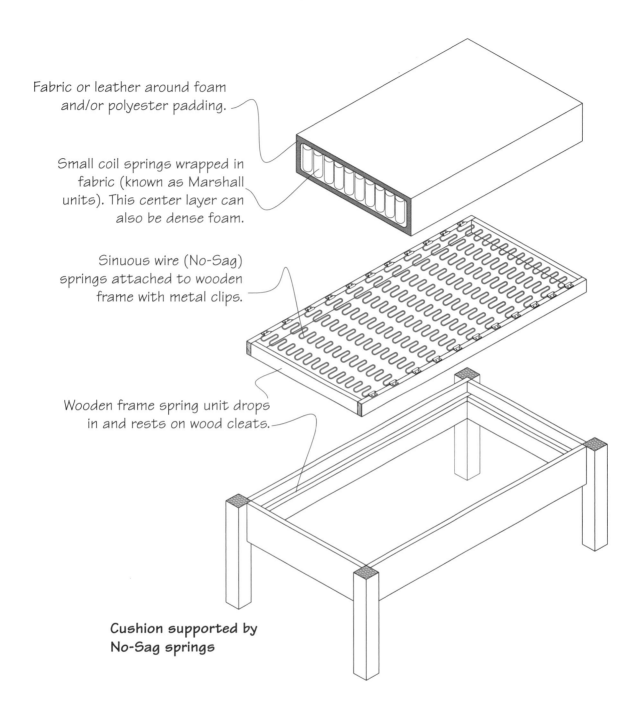

Fabric or leather around foam and/or polyester padding.

Small coil springs wrapped in fabric (known as Marshall units). This center layer can also be dense foam.

Sinuous wire (No-Sag) springs attached to wooden frame with metal clips.

Wooden frame spring unit drops in and rests on wood cleats.

Cushion supported by No-Sag springs

and a cushion placed on top. Alternatively, layers of different padding materials may be placed directly over the springs, with the final layer of leather or fabric as the layer that shows. When a load is placed on any one spring, it compresses, and the tying causes all the neighboring springs to also compress. This allows the seat to be quite comfortable, moving slightly with the sitter. It also spreads the load, resulting in longer life for both the springs and the cushions.

There are also a number of choices for cushion material. One hundred years ago, the choices weren't as numerous nor as comfortable. Horsehair, excelsior, and cotton batting were common, not only in Craftsman furniture, but also in other upholstered furniture of the period. Foam cushions did not come into use until the 1930s. Modern polyurethane foams function better than the earlier alternatives, and are available in a range of densities and thicknesses. The biggest drawback to foam cushions is that they usually take 24 hours or more to return to their uncompressed state. As time goes on, foam cushions tend to stay compressed and the seat gets harder and less resilient. Good quality cushions are usually a combination of materials with the foam wrapped in polyester or cotton batting. A layer of down adds a considerable measure of comfort, as do small, wrapped coil springs inside the cushion.

Leather was the first choice of fabric on the originals and is a good choice today, although it is expensive. It is extremely durable, looks good in combination with wood, and is very comfortable. Original cushions also were covered with heavy canvas, and today there are a variety of upholstery fabrics available that will work well with this style of furniture.

In the drawings I have tried to indicate what the original material and method of supporting the seat was, if it was possible to determine. Many times existing pieces bear no trace of their original upholstery. Pieces that were in production for several years were likely to have used different methods and materials in different years. Attempts to be authentic in building a reproduction will need to be tempered by the realization that 100% historical accuracy may not be possible. In my opinion, strict authenticity usually should take second place to issues of comfort and durability.

Building one of the large chairs or settles from the drawings in this book represents a considerable investment both in materials and in time. While those of us who work with wood tend to think that the purpose for having one of these pieces in our homes is so

that others may admire our skills, the rest of the world is looking for a comfortable place to sit and relax. The best way to admire a Morris chair is while seated in it. I think it is unwise to scrimp on materials at this point, and I have no problem in hiring someone else to do the upholstery. I have enough trouble getting the wooden parts to work without diving into materials and techniques that aren't as familiar to me.

Most of the furniture designs in this book use either a loose cushion, or can use a removable frame for springs to support the seat cushions. This is how the original furniture was made, and it is an advantage to today's woodworker. All of the wooden parts can be completely finished, then the springs or other seat supports can be installed at the very last step. This is far easier than trying to work around upholstery during finishing, and it nearly eliminates the risks of damaging the finish while doing the upholstery. The fact that these are two distinct processes makes it easier to have the work done by two distinct people.

These designs also lend themselves to trading up at some later date. If you are on a tight budget, you can use a futon, or a foam cushion supported by simple wood slats that rest on cleats inside the frame of the chair or settle. These parts are in no way permanent, so at some later time they can be replaced by a drop-in frame with spring supports. In fact the wooden structure, if carefully made, will last many times longer than any of the upholstery, no matter what choice you make initially.

DINING ROOM

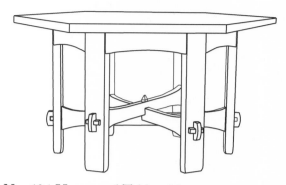

No. 624 Hexagonal Table   32

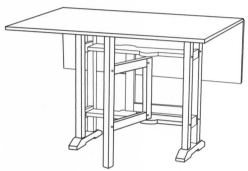

No. 552 Gate Leg Table   28

No. 800 Sideboard   40

No. 353 Side Chair 36

No. 353A Arm Chair   38

DINING ROOM

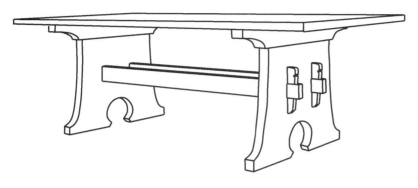

No. 599 Large Trestle Table 45

No. 962 Serving Table 56

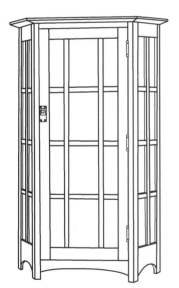

No. 719 Glass Corner Cabinet 48

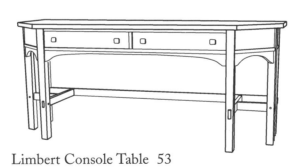

Limbert Console Table 53

No. 729 China Cabinet 60

No. 803 Harvey Ellis
China Cabinet 64

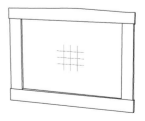

No. 66 Wall Mirror 68

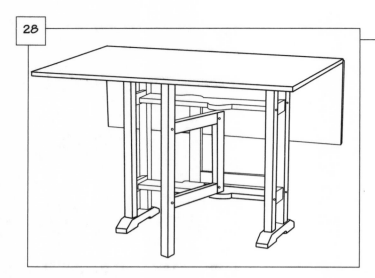

L. & J. G. STICKLEY
NO. 552 GATELEG TABLE

42 x 42 x 30 high open, 14 x 42 closed
[1067 x 1067 x 762 open, 356 x 1067 closed]

A marvelous little table. With the leaves down, it can be used behind a sofa or as an entry table. With the leaves up, it can seat four for breakfast or lunch. Great to use on the holidays for extra seating.

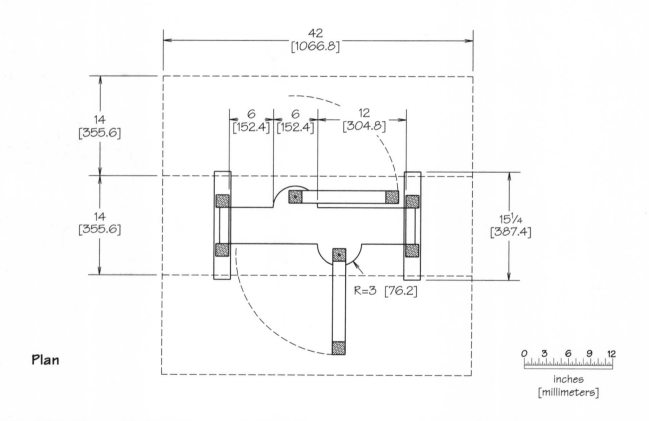

Plan

inches
[millimeters]

L. & J. G. Stickley No. 552 Gateleg Table

QTY	PART	SIZE		NOTES
1	top	$^7/_8$ x 15$^1/_2$ x 42	[22.2 x 393.7 x 1066.8]	14 [355.6] exposed between rule joints
2	leaves	$^7/_8$ x 14 x 42	[22.2 x 355.6 x 1066.8]	
4	fixed legs	1$^3/_4$ x 1$^3/_4$ x 27$^1/_4$	[44.5 x 44.5 x 692.2]	
2	feet	1$^7/_8$ x 2$^1/_4$ x 15$^1/_4$	[47.6 x 57.2 x 387.4]	
4	leg stretchers	1$^1/_4$ x 2$^1/_4$ x 7$^3/_4$	[31.8 x 57.2 x 196.9]	5$^1/_4$ [133.4] between tenons
2	top leg rails	$^7/_8$ x 1$^3/_4$ x 6$^1/_4$	[22.2 x 44.5 x 158.8]	5$^1/_4$ [133.4] between tenons
2	shelves	$^7/_8$ x 11$^1/_4$ x 25	[22.2 x 285.8 x 635]	24 [609.6] between tenons
2	pivoting legs	1$^3/_4$ x 1$^3/_4$ x 29$^1/_8$	[44.5 x 44.5 x 739.8]	
2	pivot uprights	1$^3/_4$ x 1$^3/_4$ x 14$^1/_4$	[44.5 x 44.5 x 362]	
4	pivot rails	1$^3/_4$ x 1$^3/_4$ x 13$^7/_8$	[44.5 x 44.5 x 352.4]	11$^3/_8$ [288.9] between tenons

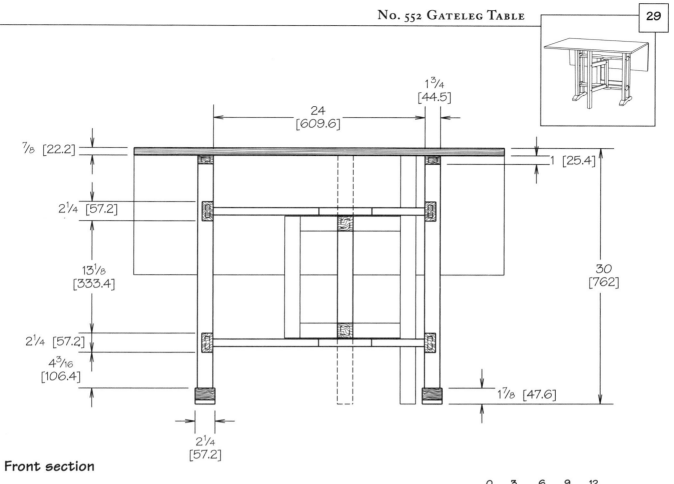

$\frac{7}{8}$ [22.2]

$2\frac{1}{4}$ [57.2]

$13\frac{1}{8}$ [333.4]

$2\frac{1}{4}$ [57.2]

$4\frac{3}{16}$ [106.4]

24 [609.6]

$1\frac{3}{4}$ [44.5]

1 [25.4]

30 [762]

$1\frac{7}{8}$ [47.6]

$2\frac{1}{4}$ [57.2]

Front section

0   3   6   9   12
inches
[millimeters]

$8\frac{3}{4}$ [222.3]

$1\frac{3}{4}$ [44.5]

$27\frac{1}{4}$ [692.2]

5 [127]

$15\frac{1}{4}$ [387.4]

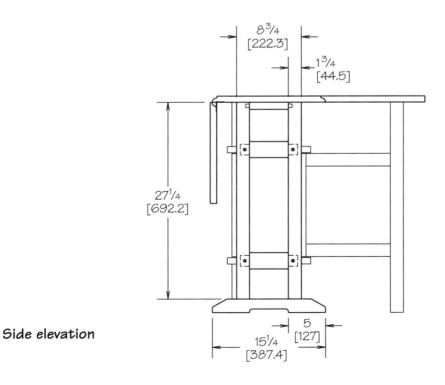

Side elevation

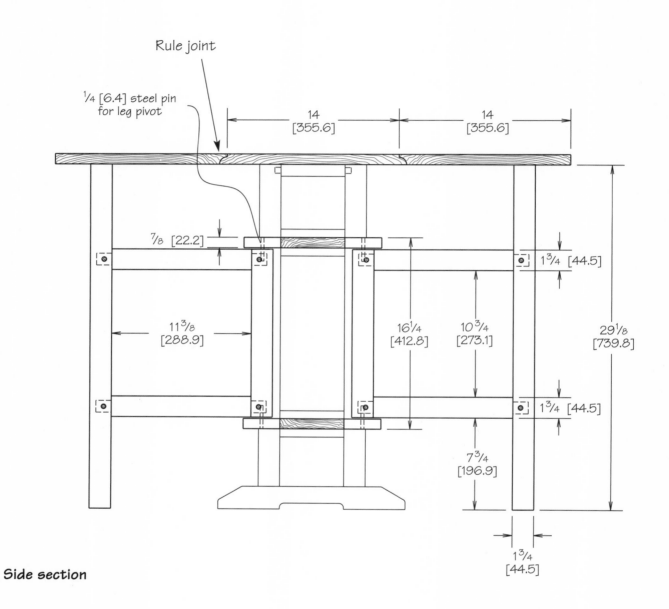

Rule joint

$1/4$ [6.4] steel pin
for leg pivot

14
[355.6]

14
[355.6]

$7/8$ [22.2]

$11^3/8$
[288.9]

$16^1/4$
[412.8]

$10^3/4$
[273.1]

$1^3/4$ [44.5]

$1^3/4$ [44.5]

$29^1/8$
[739.8]

$7^3/4$
[196.9]

$1^3/4$
[44.5]

Side section

Foot detail

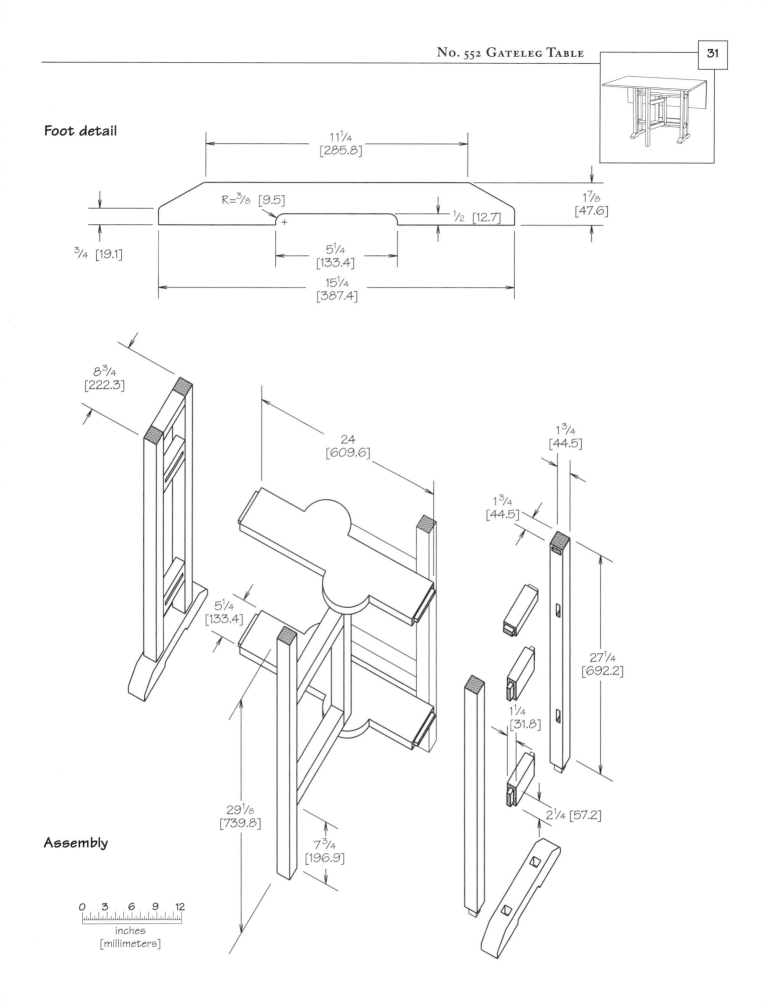

11¼
[285.8]

R=³⁄₈ [9.5]

1⁷⁄₈
[47.6]

½ [12.7]

³⁄₄ [19.1]

5¼
[133.4]

15¼
[387.4]

8³⁄₄
[222.3]

24
[609.6]

1³⁄₄
[44.5]

1³⁄₄
[44.5]

5¼
[133.4]

27¼
[692.2]

1¼
[31.8]

29⅛
[739.8]

7³⁄₄
[196.9]

2¼ [57.2]

Assembly

0 3 6 9 12

inches
[millimeters]

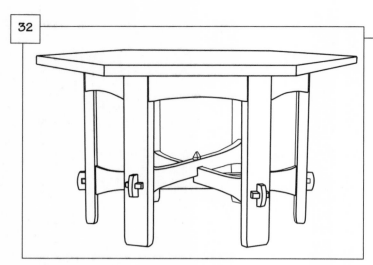

GUSTAV STICKLEY
NO. 624 HEXAGONAL TABLE
48 x 29 high [1219 x 737 high]

This was listed as a library table, and often seen with a leather top. The design was simplified in later years, the keyed tenons disappeared, and the stretchers were unstacked. Do a full size layout of the central joint of the stretchers to determine the locations of the lap joints, which are pinned.

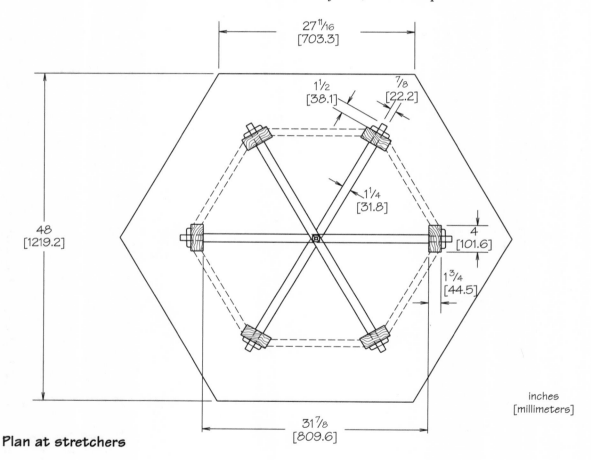

Plan at stretchers

Gustav Stickley No. 624 Hexagonal Table

QTY	PART	SIZE		NOTES
1	top	1⁵⁄₈ x 48 x 55⁷⁄₁₆	[41.3 x 1219.2 x 1408.1]	
6	legs	1³⁄₄ x 4 x 27³⁄₈	[44.5 x 101.6 x 695.3]	
3	stretchers	1¹⁄₄ x 4¹⁄₂ x 38¹⁄₂	[31.8 x 114.3 x 977.9]	31⁷⁄₈ [806.5] between tenons
6	aprons	1 x 4 x 13⁷⁄₈	[25.4 x 101.6 x 352.4]	exposed—add for tenons
6	keys	⁵⁄₈ x ¹⁵⁄₁₆ x 2⁷⁄₈	[15.9 x 23.8 x 73]	
1	pin	1 x 1 x 5¹⁄₄	[25.4 x 25.4 x 133.4]	¹⁄₂ [12.7] diameter turned end

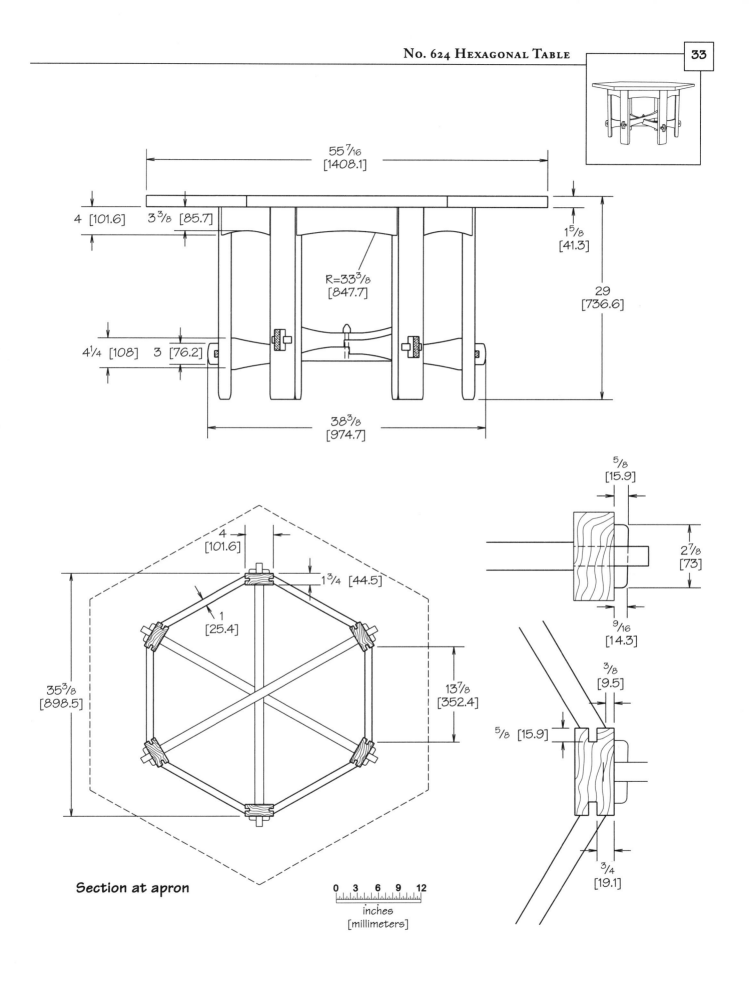

55⁷/₁₆
[1408.1]

4 [101.6]

3³/₈ [85.7]

R=33³/₈
[847.7]

1⁵/₈
[41.3]

29
[736.6]

4¹/₄ [108]   3 [76.2]

38³/₈
[974.7]

5/₈
[15.9]

2⁷/₈
[73]

9/₁₆
[14.3]

4
[101.6]

1³/₄ [44.5]

1
[25.4]

35³/₈
[898.5]

13⁷/₈
[352.4]

3/₈
[9.5]

5/₈ [15.9]

3/₄
[19.1]

Section at apron

0 3 6 9 12
inches
[millimeters]

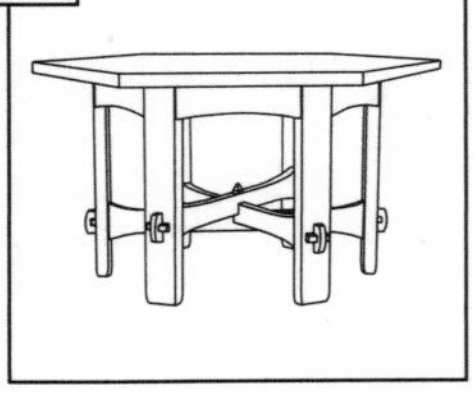

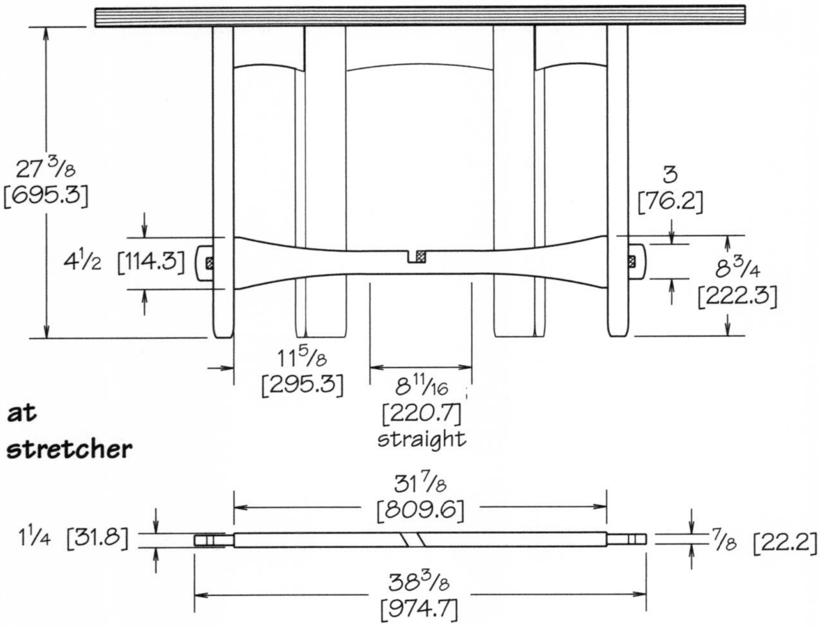

27 3/8
[695.3]

4 1/2 [114.3]

3
[76.2]

8 3/4
[222.3]

11 5/8
[295.3]

8 11/16
[220.7]
straight

**Section at
bottom stretcher**

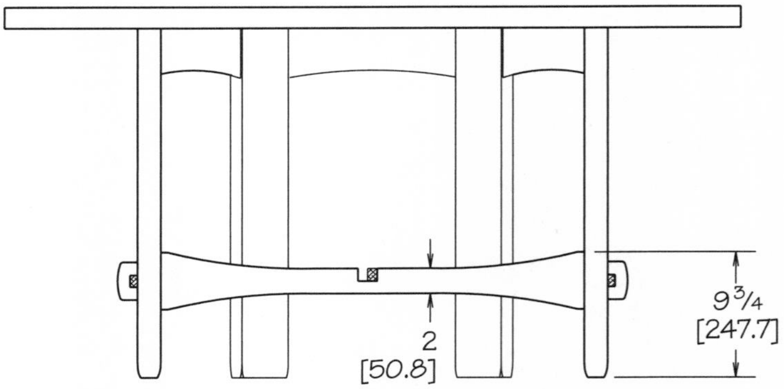

31 7/8
[809.6]

1 1/4 [31.8]

7/8 [22.2]

38 3/8
[974.7]

Section at middle stretcher

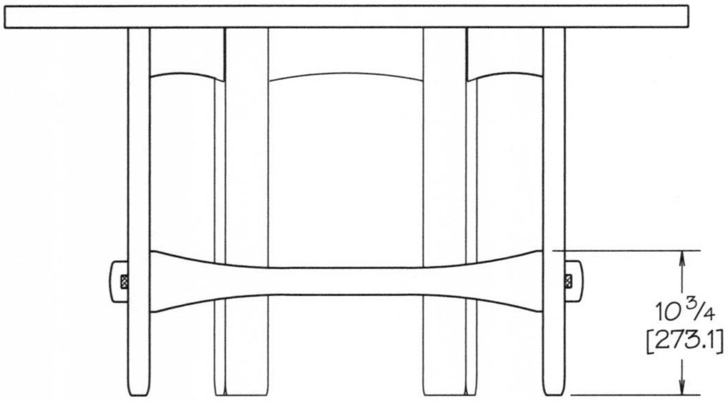

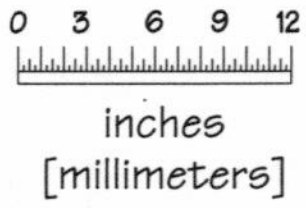

9 3/4
[247.7]

2
[50.8]

10 3/4
[273.1]

0   3   6   9   12

inches
[millimeters]

Section at top stretcher

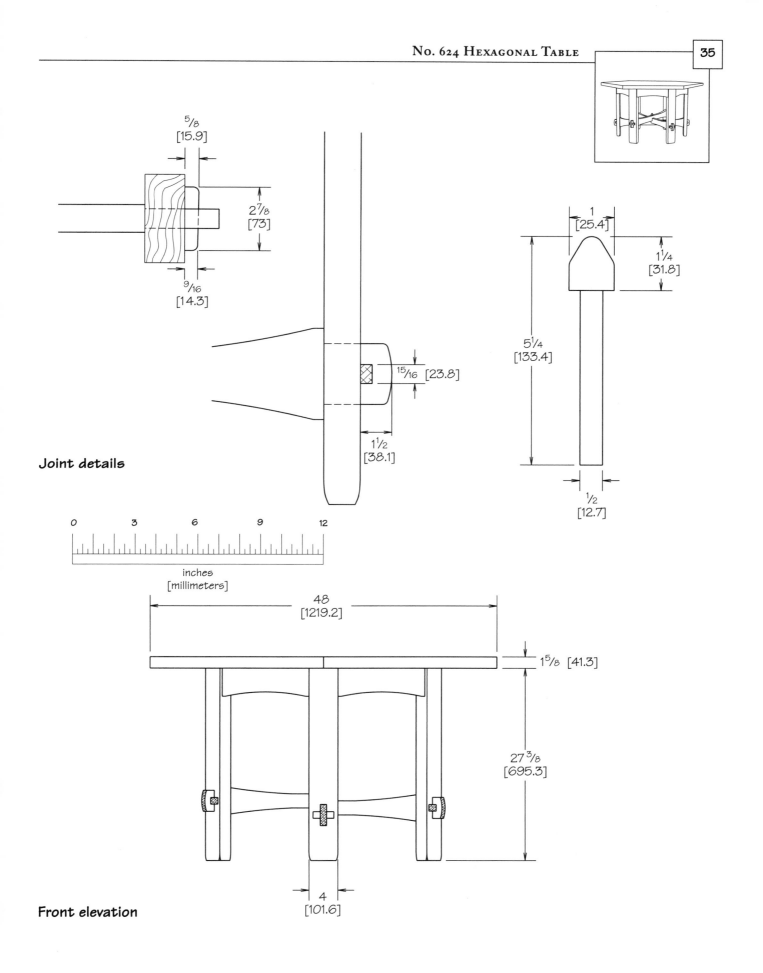

⁵/₈
[15.9]

2⁷/₈
[73]

⁹/₁₆
[14.3]

1
[25.4]

1¹/₄
[31.8]

5¹/₄
[133.4]

¹/₂
[12.7]

¹⁵/₁₆ [23.8]

1¹/₂
[38.1]

Joint details

0   3   6   9   12

inches
[millimeters]

48
[1219.2]

1⁵/₈ [41.3]

27³/₈
[695.3]

4
[101.6]

Front elevation

GUSTAV STICKLEY
NO. 353 SIDE CHAIR
NO. 353A ARM CHAIR

The seat cushion is a slip seat — either a hardwood frame, or a piece of plywood covered with padding and then wrapped with fabric. After the chair is finished, the completed seat is attached with screws through the corner blocks from underneath.

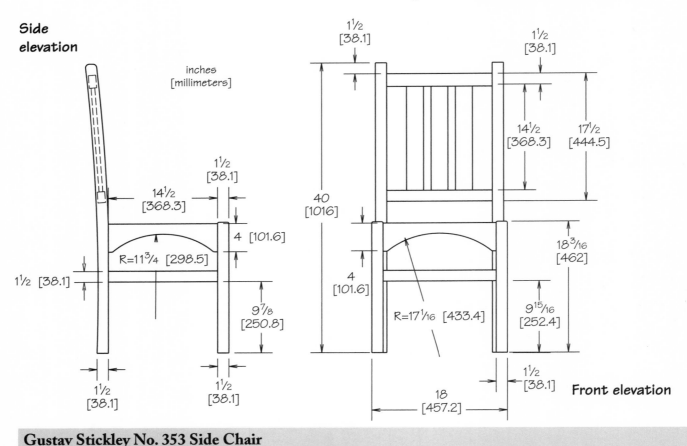

Side elevation

inches [millimeters]

1½ [38.1]
1½ [38.1]
14½ [368.3]
1½ [38.1]
4 [101.6]
R=11³⁄₄ [298.5]
1½ [38.1]
9⁷⁄₈ [250.8]
1½ [38.1]
1½ [38.1]

1½ [38.1]
1½ [38.1]
14½ [368.3]
17½ [444.5]
40 [1016]
4 [101.6]
18³⁄₁₆ [462]
R=17¹⁄₁₆ [433.4]
9¹⁵⁄₁₆ [252.4]
1½ [38.1]
18 [457.2]

Front elevation

Gustav Stickley No. 353 Side Chair

QTY	PART	SIZE		NOTES
2	front legs	1½ x 1½ x 18³⁄₁₆	[38.1 x 38.1 x 462]	
2	back legs	1½ x 3 x 40	[38.1 x 76.2 x 1016]	
1	lower front rail	³⁄₄ x 1½ x 16	[19.1 x 38.1 x 406.4]	15 [381] between tenons
1	arched front rail	1 x 4 x 16	[25.4 x 101.6 x 406.4]	15 [381] between tenons
1	lower back rail	³⁄₄ x 1½ x 15	[19.1 x 38.1 x 381]	14 [355.6] between tenons
1	arched back rail	1 x 4 x 15	[25.4 x 101.6 x 381]	14 [355.6] between tenons
2	lower side rails	³⁄₄ x 1½ x 15½	[19.1 x 38.1 x 393.7]	14½ [368.3] between tenons
2	arched side rails	1 x 4 x 15½	[25.4 x 101.6 x 393.7]	14½ [368.3] between tenons
1	top curved back rail	1 x 1³⁄₄ x 15	[25.4 x 44.5 x 381]	14 [355.6] betw tenons make longer for bending
1	bot. curved back rail	1 x 1½ x 15	[25.4 x 38.1 x 381]	14 [355.6] betw tenons make longer for bending
3	back slats	½ x 2¹⁄₄ x 15⁵⁄₁₆	[12.7 x 57.2 x 388.9]	14⁵⁄₁₆ [363.5] between tenons

Plan section at seat

Side section

17
[431.8]

1½
[38.1]

17½
[444.5]

2¼
[57.2]

1
[25.4]

1
[25.4]

R=32⁷⁄₈ [835.0]

**Plan section
through back**

0 3 6 9 12
inches
[millimeters]

1
[25.4]

1³⁄₄
[44.5]

17⁹⁄₁₆
[446.1]

1½
[38.1]

3⁄₈
[9.5]

4
[101.6]

2³⁄₄ [69.9]

R=11³⁄₄ [298.5]

1½ [38.1]

1 [25.4]

3
[76.2]

14½
[368.3]

17
[431.8]

88°

1½ [38.1]

1½
[38.1]

18
[457.2]

Plan

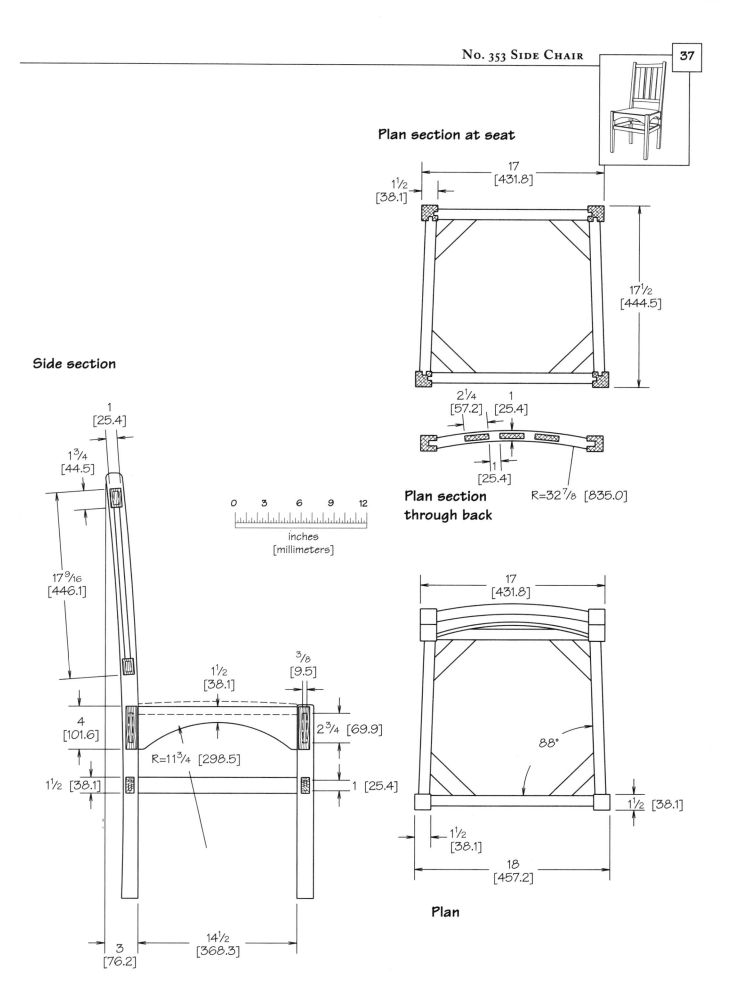

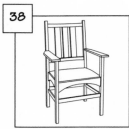

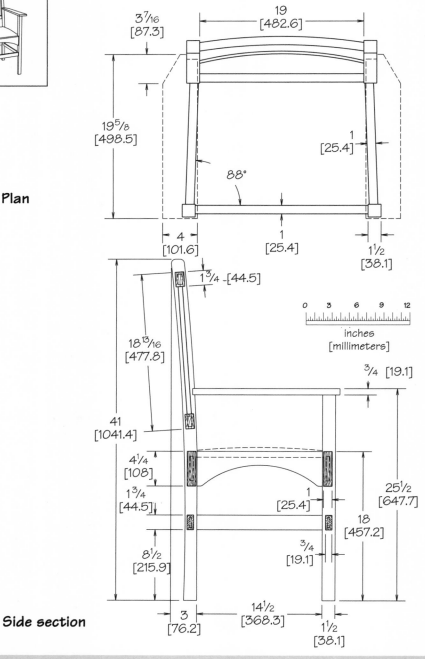

Plan

Side section

Gustav Stickley No. 353A Arm Chair

QTY	PART	SIZE		NOTES
2	front legs	1½ x 1½ x 25⅞	[38.1 x 38.1 x 657.2]	25½ [647.7] below arm
2	back legs	1½ x 3 x 41	[38.1 x 76.2 x 1041.4]	
1	lower front rail	¾ x 1¾ x 21	[19.1 x 44.5 x 533.4]	20 [508] between tenons
1	arched front rail	1 x 4¼ x 21	[25.4 x 108 x 533.4]	20 [508] between tenons
1	lower back rail	¾ x 1¾ x 20	[19.1 x 44.5 x 508]	19 [482.6] between tenons
1	arched back rail	1 x 4¼ x 20	[25.4 x 108 x 508]	19 [482.6] between tenons
2	lower side rails	¾ x 1¾ x 15½	[19.1 x 44.5 x 393.7]	14½ [368.3] between tenons
2	arched side rails	1 x 4½ x 15½	[25.4 x 114.3 x 393.7]	14½ [368.3] between tenons
2	curved back rails	1 x 1¾ x 20½	[25.4 x 44.5 x 520.7]	19 [482.6] between tenons-make longer for bending
3	back slats	½ x 2¾ x 16⁵⁄₁₆	[12.7 x 69.9 x 414.3]	15⁵⁄₁₆ [388.9] between tenons
2	arms	¾ x 4 x 19⅝	[19.1 x 101.6 x 498.5]	

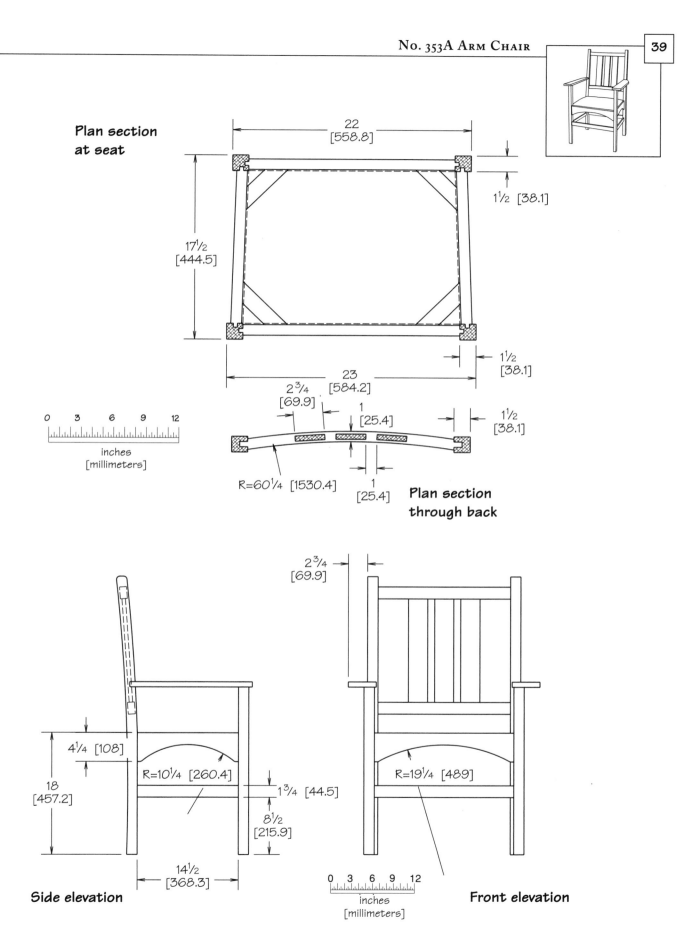

Plan section at seat

22 [558.8]

1½ [38.1]

17½ [444.5]

1½ [38.1]

23 [584.2]

0 3 6 9 12

inches [millimeters]

2³/₄ [69.9]

1 [25.4]

1½ [38.1]

R=60¼ [1530.4]

1 [25.4]

Plan section through back

2³/₄ [69.9]

4¼ [108]

R=10¼ [260.4]

1³/₄ [44.5]

18 [457.2]

8½ [215.9]

14½ [368.3]

Side elevation

R=19¼ [489]

0 3 6 9 12

inches [millimeters]

Front elevation

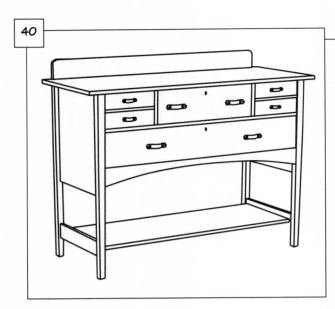

GUSTAV STICKLEY
NO. 800 SIDEBOARD

39 high x 54 wide x 21 deep [991 x 1372 x 533]

Originally produced in 1903, this Harvey Ellis design is much lighter in feel than many Stickley pieces, while providing a good deal of storage in a relatively small space.

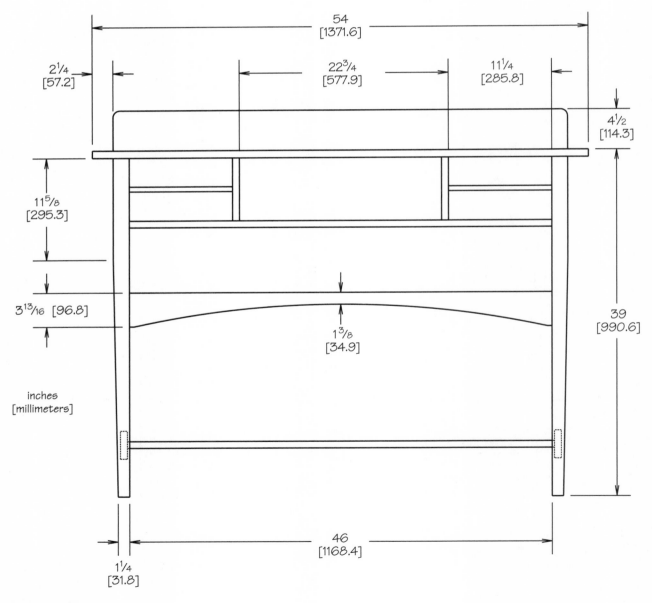

54
[1371.6]

2¼
[57.2]

22³/₄
[577.9]

11¼
[285.8]

4½
[114.3]

11⁵/₈
[295.3]

3¹³/₁₆ [96.8]

1³/₈
[34.9]

39
[990.6]

inches
[millimeters]

46
[1168.4]

1¼
[31.8]

Front elevation

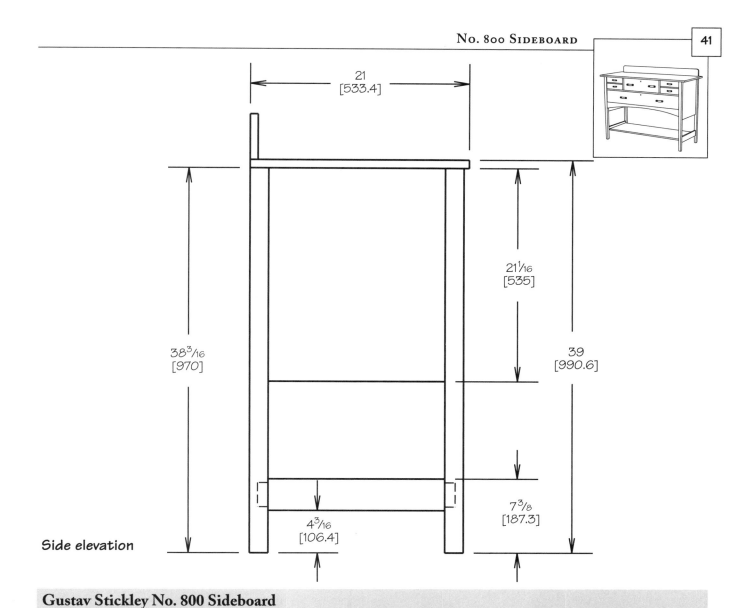

Side elevation

Dimensions shown: 21 [533.4], 21¹/₁₆ [535], 38³/₁₆ [970], 39 [990.6], 7³/₈ [187.3], 4³/₁₆ [106.4]

Gustav Stickley No. 800 Sideboard

Qty	Part	Size		Notes
4	legs	1³/₄ x 1³/₄ x 38³/₁₆	[44.5 x 44.5 x 970]	
1	top	¹³/₁₆ x 21 x 54	[20.6 x 533.4 x 1371.6]	
1	backsplash	³/₄ x 4¹/₂ x 49¹/₂	[19.1 x 114.3 x 1257.3]	
2	side stretchers	³/₄ x 3¹/₈ x 19	[19.1 x 79.4 x 482.6]	17 [431.8] tenons
1	shelf	³/₄ x 15⁷/₈ x 47¹/₄	[19.1 x 403.2 x 1200.2]	46¹/₂ [1181.1] between tenons
2	side panels	³/₄ x 17³/₄ x 21¹/₁₆	[19.1 x 450.9 x 535]	17 [431.8] exposed
1	back panel	³/₄ x 16¹/₂ x 46³/₄	[19.1 x 419.1 x 1187.5]	46 [1168.4] exposed
1	shelf below drawers	³/₄ x 19¹/₂ x 46³/₄	[19.1 x 495.3 x 1187.5]	
1	arched front apron	³/₄ x 3¹³/₁₆ x 47	[19.1 x 96.8 x 1193.8]	46 [1168.4] between tenons
1	front rail	³/₄ x 2 x 46¹/₂	[19.1 x 50.8 x 1181.1]	46 [1168.4] between tenons
2	drawer rails	⁵/₈ x 2 x 11³/₄	[15.9 x 50.8 x 298.5]	11¹/₄ [285.8] between tenons
2	drawer dividers	³/₄ x 2 x 7³/₁₆	[19.1 x 50.8 x 182.6]	
1	bottom drawer front	³/₄ x 7³/₈ x 46	[19.1 x 187.3 x 1168.4]	opening
1	center drawer front	³/₄ x 7³/₁₆ x 22	[19.1 x 182.6 x 558.8]	opening
2	drawer fronts	³/₄ x 3³/₈ x 11¹/₄	[19. x 85.7 x 295.8]	opening
2	drawer fronts	³/₄ x 3¹/₈ x 11¹/₄	[19.1 x 79.4 x 295.8]	opening

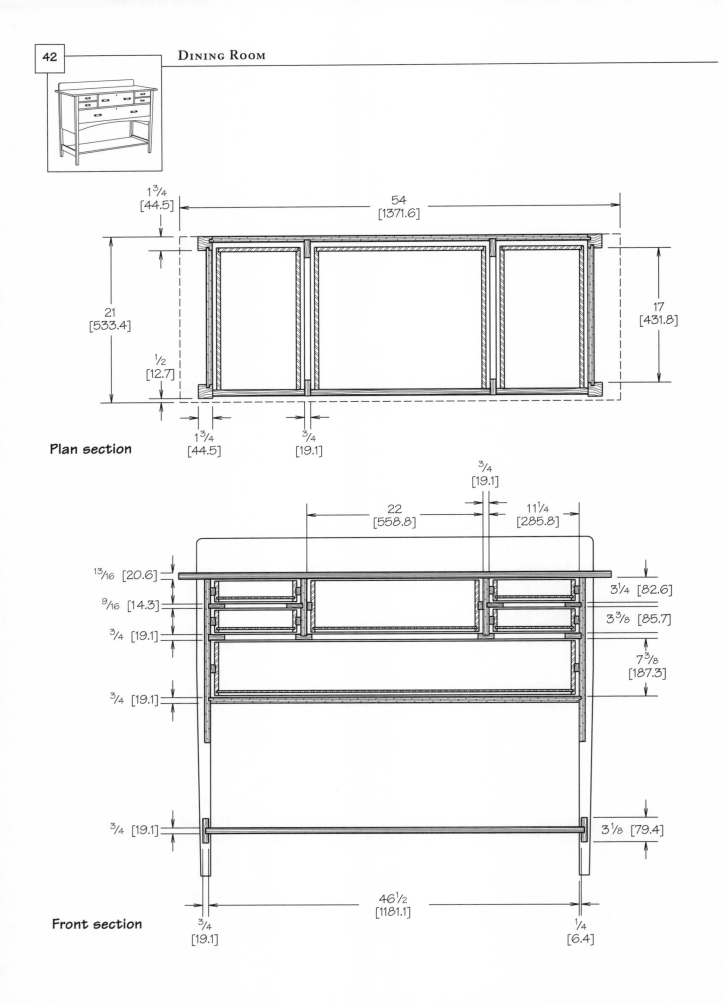

1³/₄
[44.5]

54
[1371.6]

21
[533.4]

17
[431.8]

¹/₂
[12.7]

Plan section

1³/₄
[44.5]

³/₄
[19.1]

³/₄
[19.1]

22
[558.8]

11¹/₄
[285.8]

13/16 [20.6]

³/₄ [82.6]

9/16 [14.3]

3³/₈ [85.7]

³/₄ [19.1]

7³/₈
[187.3]

³/₄ [19.1]

³/₄ [19.1]

3¹/₈ [79.4]

46¹/₂
[1181.1]

Front section

³/₄
[19.1]

¹/₄
[6.4]

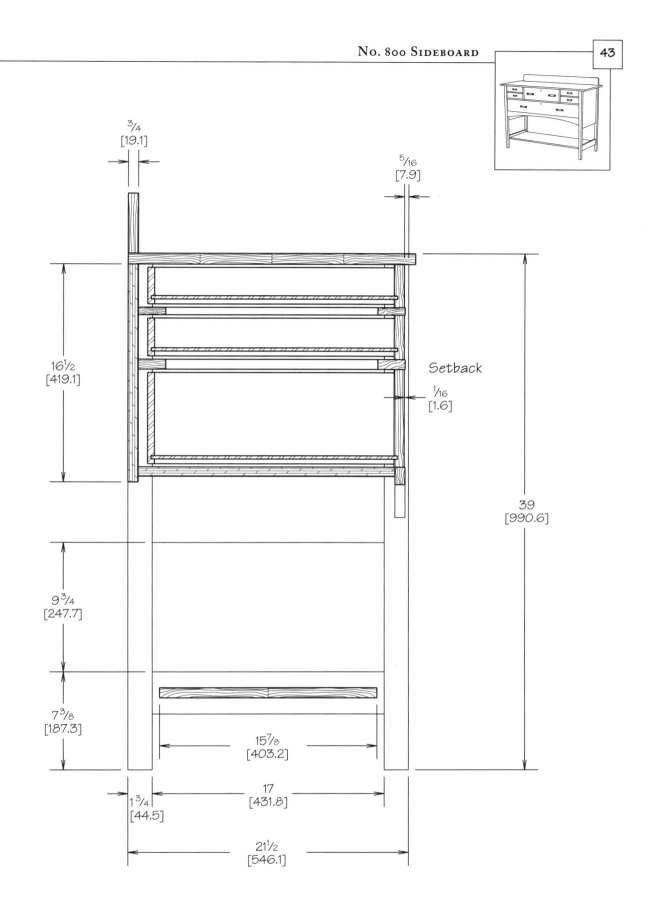

3/4
[19.1]

5/16
[7.9]

16¹/₂
[419.1]

Setback

1/16
[1.6]

39
[990.6]

9³/₄
[247.7]

7³/₈
[187.3]

15⁷/₈
[403.2]

17
[431.8]

1³/₄
[44.5]

21¹/₂
[546.1]

Side section

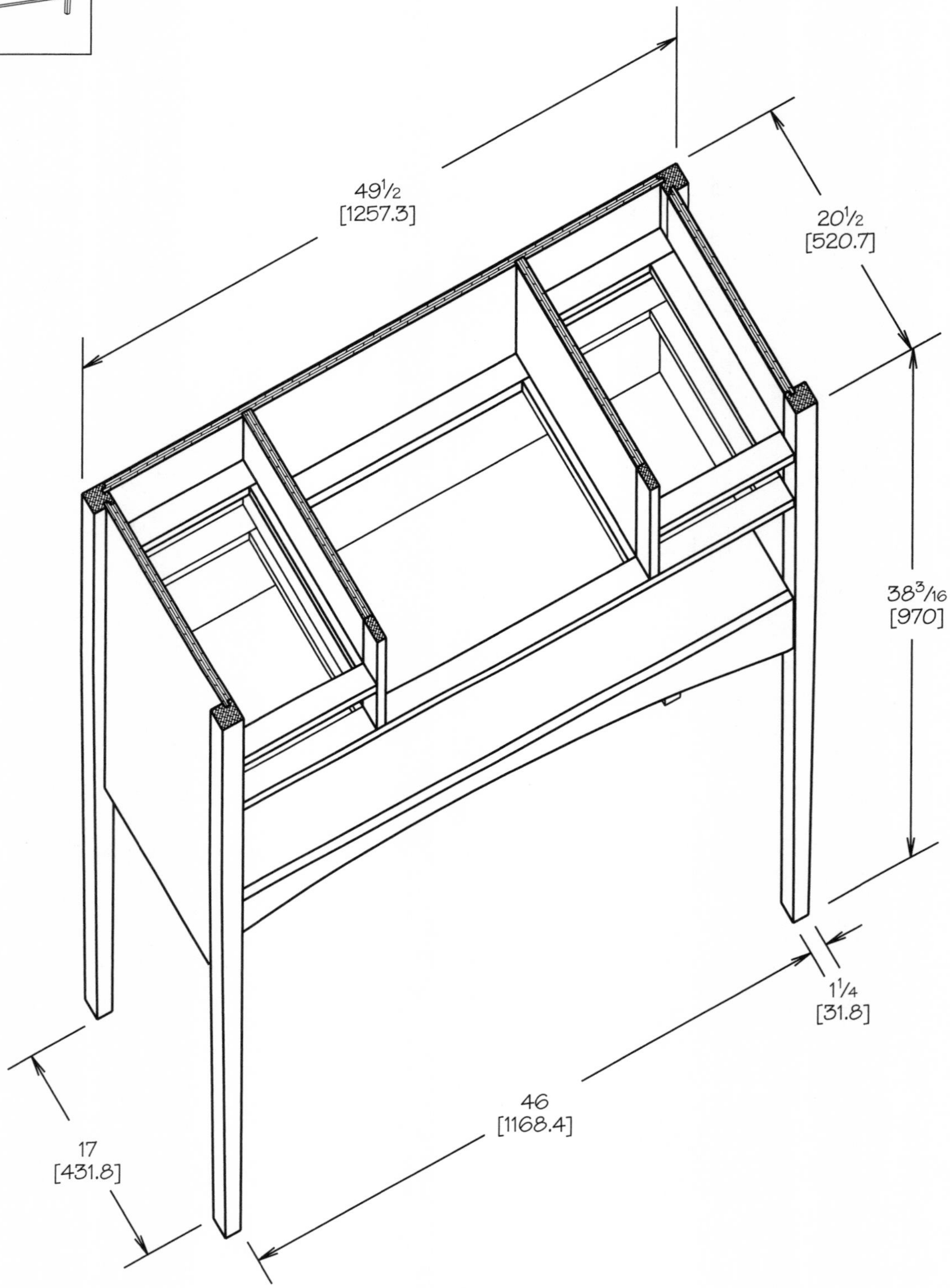

49¹/₂
[1257.3]

20¹/₂
[520.7]

38³/₁₆
[970]

1¹/₄
[31.8]

46
[1168.4]

17
[431.8]

Assembly

L. & J. G. STICKLEY
NO. 599 TRESTLE TABLE

29 high x 42 x 84 [737 high x 1067 x 2134]

A massive Arts & Crafts style table. The construction is obvious, so no section views are really needed. Large screws through oversized holes in the top rails attach the top.

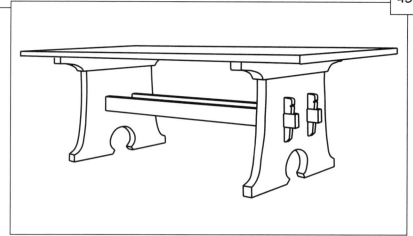

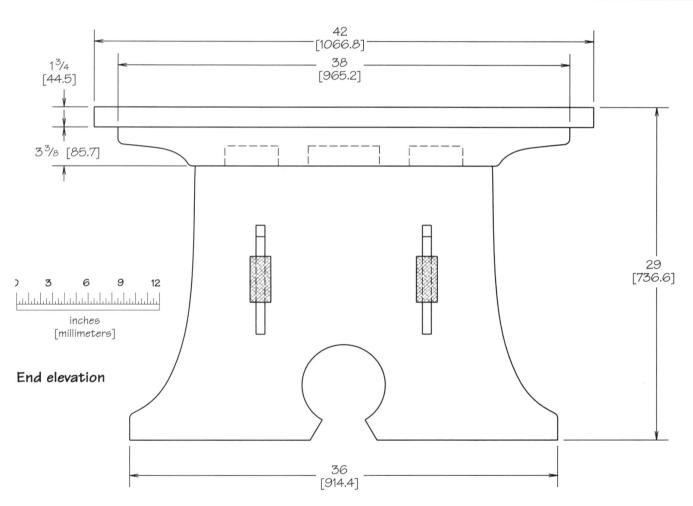

End elevation

inches
[millimeters]

L. & J. G. Stickley No. 599 Trestle Table

QTY	PART	SIZE		NOTES
1	top	1³/₄ x 42 x 84	[44.5 x 1066.8 x 2133.6]	
2	ends	2¹/₄ x 36 x 25³/₄	[57.2 x 914.4 x 654.1]	23⁷/₈ [606.4] exposed
2	end rails	2³/₄ x 3³/₈ x 38	[69.9 x 85.7 x 965.2]	
2	stretchers	2¹/₄ x 4 x 62¹/₄	[57.2 x 101.6 x 1581.2]	51 [1295.4] between tenons
4	keys	³/₄ x 1⁷/₈ x 9¹/₂	[19.1 x 47.6 x 241.3]	

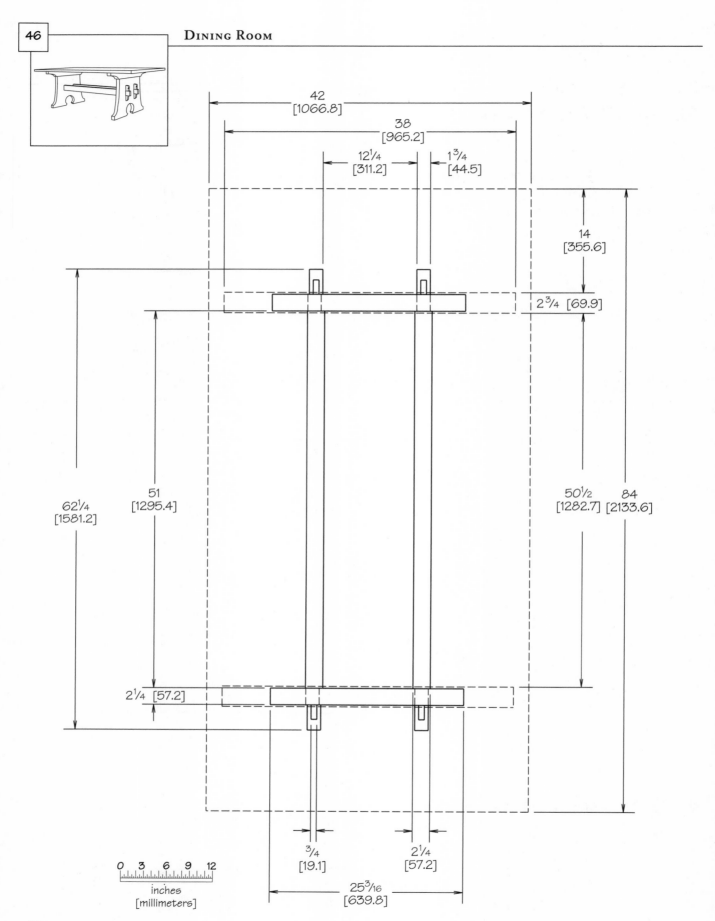

42
[1066.8]

38
[965.2]

12¼
[311.2]

1¾
[44.5]

14
[355.6]

2¾ [69.9]

51
[1295.4]

62¼
[1581.2]

50½
[1282.7]

84
[2133.6]

2¼ [57.2]

¾
[19.1]

2¼
[57.2]

0 3 6 9 12

inches
[millimeters]

25³⁄₁₆
[639.8]

Plan

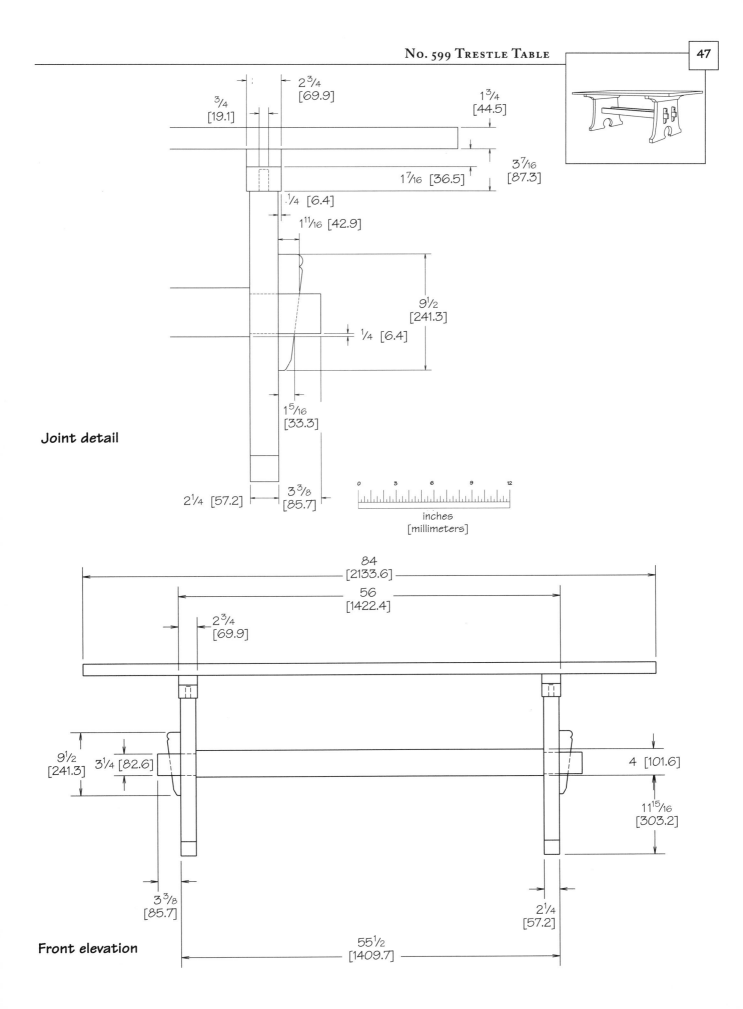

3/4
[19.1]

2 3/4
[69.9]

1 3/4
[44.5]

3 7/16
[87.3]

1 7/16 [36.5]

1/4 [6.4]

1 11/16 [42.9]

9 1/2
[241.3]

1/4 [6.4]

1 5/16
[33.3]

2 1/4 [57.2]

3 3/8
[85.7]

Joint detail

0   3   6   9   12

inches
[millimeters]

84
[2133.6]

56
[1422.4]

2 3/4
[69.9]

9 1/2
[241.3]

3 1/4 [82.6]

4 [101.6]

11 15/16
[303.2]

3 3/8
[85.7]

2 1/4
[57.2]

55 1/2
[1409.7]

Front elevation

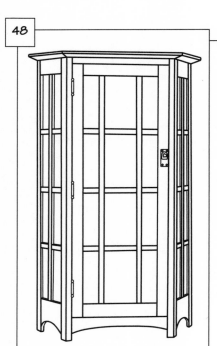

L. & J. G. STICKLEY
NO. 719 CORNER CHINA CABINET
65 high x 48 wide x 26 deep [1651 x 1219 x 660]

The shiplap back panels are rabbetted top and bottom to fit within the frame as shown in the three dimensional view. The top attaches to this frame with table irons. Use substantial hinges on the door, since it will be heavy and wide.

Note that the side sections are taken on two different cutting planes.

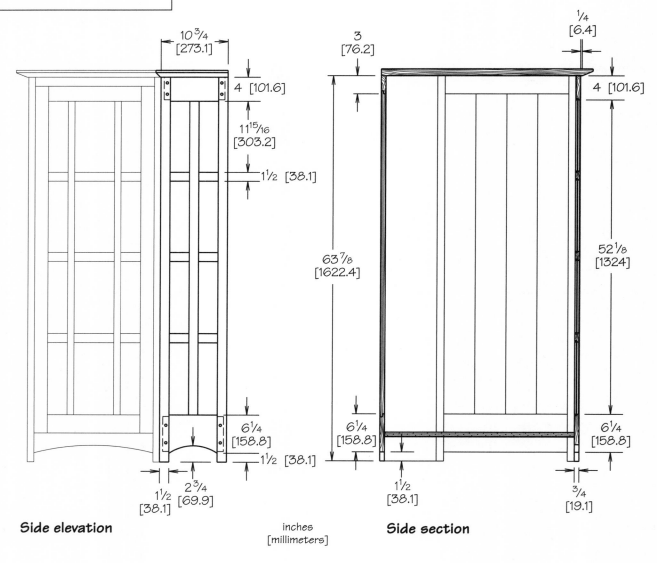

Side elevation

inches
[millimeters]

Side section

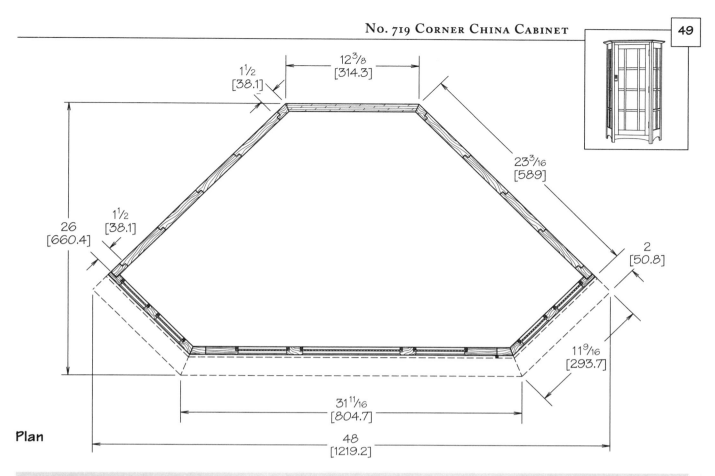

Plan

L. & J. G. Stickley No. 719 Corner China Cabinet

QTY	PART	SIZE		NOTES
2	glass panels	$3/4$ x $10^3/4$ x $63^7/8$	[19.1 x 273.1 x 1622.4]	assembled-parts detailed below
4	stiles	$3/4$ x $1^1/2$ x $63^7/8$	[19.1 x 38.1 x 1622.4]	
2	bottom rails	$3/4$ x $6^1/4$ x $9^3/4$	[19.1 x 158.8 x 247.7]	$7^3/4$ [196.9] between tenons
2	top rails	$3/4$ x 4 x $9^3/4$	[19.1 x 101.6 x 247.7]	$7^3/4$ [196.9] between tenons
2	mullions	$3/4$ x $1^1/2$ x $53^1/8$	[19.1 x 38.1 x 1349.4]	$52^1/8$ [1324] between tenons
12	muntin	$3/4$ x $1^1/2$ x $4^1/8$	[19.1 x 38.1 x 104.8]	$3^1/8$ [79.4] between tenons
1	door	$3/4$ x 27 x $57^5/8$	[19.1 x 685.8 x 1463.7]	opening size-parts detailed below
2	stiles	$3/4$ x 3 x $57^5/8$	[19.1 x 76.2 x 1463.7]	
1	bottom rail	$3/4$ x 3 x 23	[19.1 x 76.2 x 584.2]	21 [533.4] between tenons
1	top rail	$3/4$ x $2^1/2$ x 23	[19.1 x 63.5 x 584.2]	21 [533.4] between tenons
2	mullions	$3/4$ x $1^1/2$ x $53^1/8$	[19.1 x 38.1 x 1349.4]	$52^1/8$ [1324] between tenons
3	center muntins	$3/4$ x $1^1/2$ x 10	[19.1 x 38.1 x 254]	9 [228.6] between tenons
6	side muntins	$3/4$ x $1^1/2$ x $5^1/2$	[19.1 x 38.1 x 139.7]	$4^1/2$ [114.3] between tenons
6	cabinet stiles	$3/4$ x $1^1/2$ $63^7/8$	[19.1 x 38.1 x 1622.4]	
2	back bottom rails	$3/4$ x $6^1/4$ x $20^9/16$	[19.1 x 158.8 x 522.3]	
2	back top rails	$3/4$ x 3 x $20^9/16$	[19.1 x 76.2 x 522.3]	
1	front bottom rail	$3/4$ x $3^1/4$ x 29	[19.1 x 76.2 x 736.6]	27 [685.8] between tenons
1	front top rail	$3/4$ x $1^1/2$ x 29	[19.1 x 38.1 x 736.6]	27 [685.8] between tenons
1	back	$3/4$ x $12^3/8$ x $63^7/8$	[19.1 x 314.3 x 1622.4]	
8	back planks	$3/4$ x $5^5/16$ x $53^7/8$	[19.1 x 134.9 x 1368.4]	
1	bottom	$3/4$ x $22^1/2$ x $43^1/16$	[19.1 x 571.5 x 1093.8]	
3	shelves	$3/4$ x $22^1/4$ x $43^1/16$	[19.1 x 565.2 x 1093.8]	opening
1	top	$1^1/8$ x 26 x 48	[28.6 x 660.4 x 1219.2]	

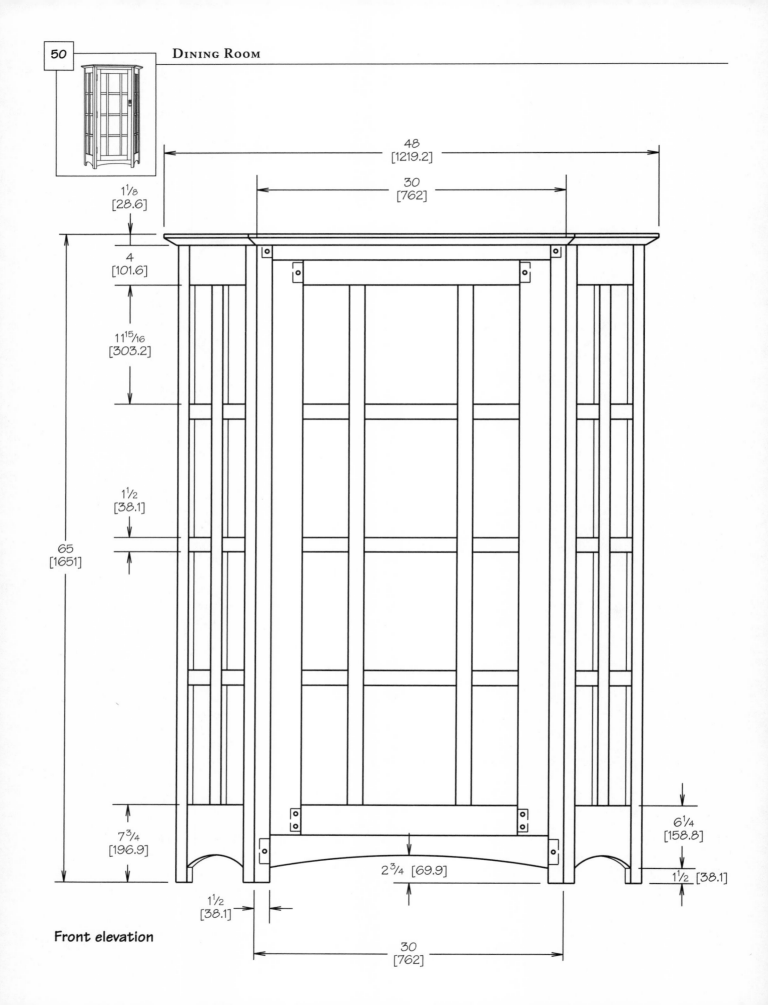

48
[1219.2]

30
[762]

1⅛
[28.6]

4
[101.6]

11¹⁵⁄₁₆
[303.2]

1½
[38.1]

65
[1651]

7¾
[196.9]

6¼
[158.8]

1½ [38.1]

2³⁄₄ [69.9]

1½
[38.1]

Front elevation

30
[762]

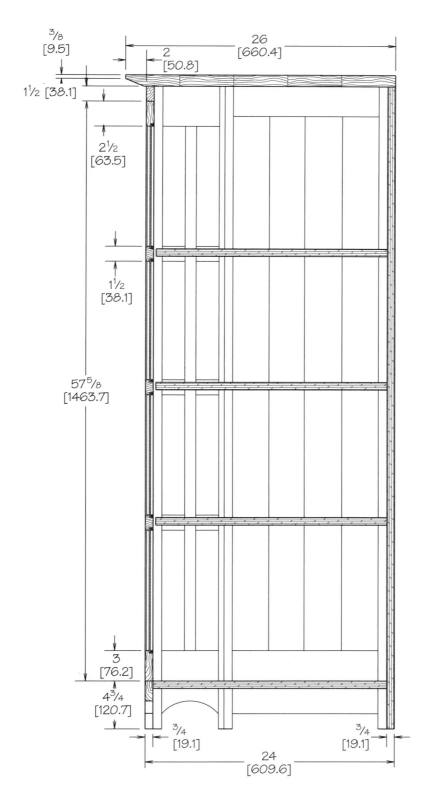

3/8
[9.5]

2
[50.8]

26
[660.4]

1½ [38.1]

2½
[63.5]

1½
[38.1]

57⅝
[1463.7]

3
[76.2]

4¾
[120.7]

3/4
[19.1]

3/4
[19.1]

24
[609.6]

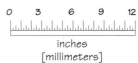

0   3   6   9   12

inches
[millimeters]

Section

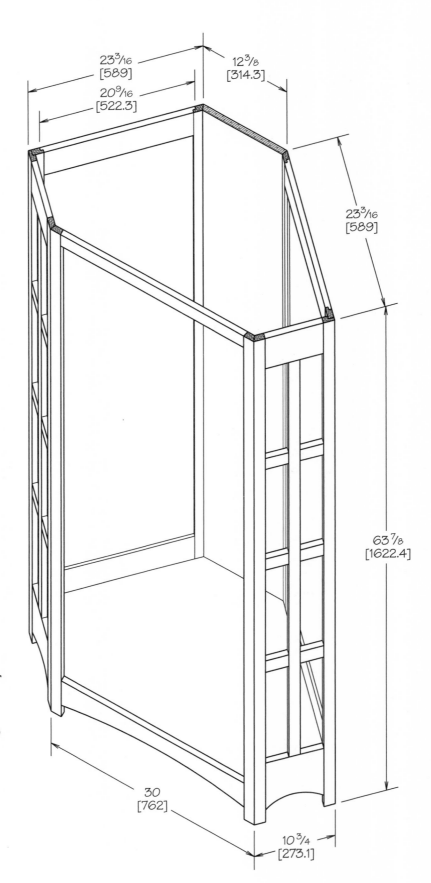

23³⁄₁₆ [589]

12³⁄₈ [314.3]

20⁹⁄₁₆ [522.3]

23³⁄₁₆ [589]

63⁷⁄₈ [1622.4]

30 [762]

10³⁄₄ [273.1]

Assemble back as open frame, and attach ship-lap back after finishing. Shelves may be permanently fastened in line with the mullions, or allowed to sit on pegs in bored holes.

Assembly

Limbert Console Table
66 wide x 21 deep x 29 high [1676 x 533 x 737]

The 3/4" [19.1] wide strip below the drawers is applied, 1/8" [3.2] thick, attached with small brads.

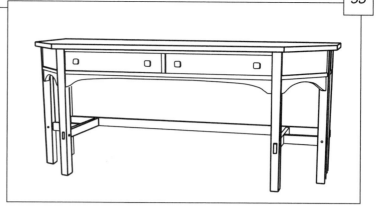

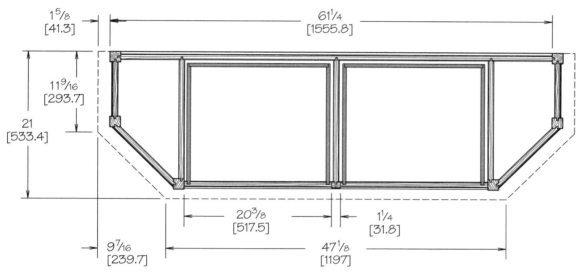

1⁵/₈ [41.3]

61¼ [1555.8]

11⁹/₁₆ [293.7]

21 [533.4]

20³/₈ [517.5]

1¼ [31.8]

9⁷/₁₆ [239.7]

47⅛ [1197]

**Plan section
through drawers**

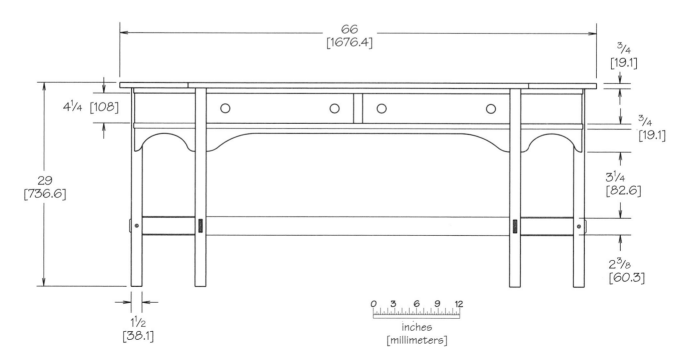

66 [1676.4]

³/₄ [19.1]

4¼ [108]

³/₄ [19.1]

3¼ [82.6]

29 [736.6]

2³/₈ [60.3]

1½ [38.1]

0 3 6 9 12
inches
[millimeters]

Front elevation

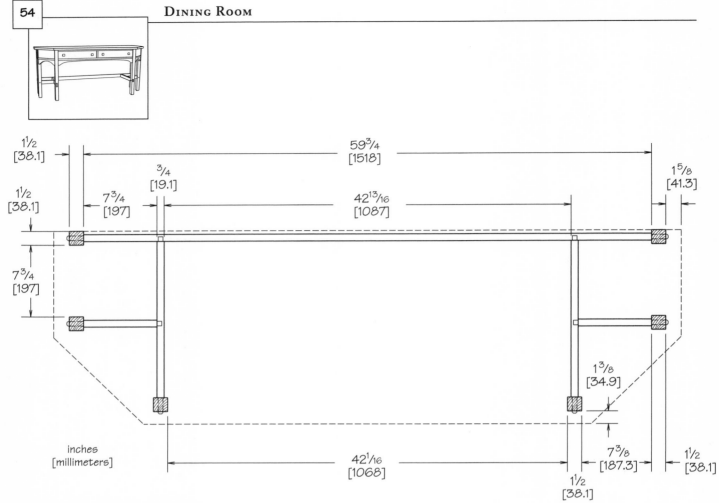

Plan section above stretchers

Limbert Console Table

QTY	PART	SIZE		NOTES
1	top	$^3/_4$ x 21 x 66	[19.1 x 533.4 x 1676.4]	
6	legs	$1^1/_2$ x $1^1/_2$ x $28^1/_4$	[38.1 x 38.1 x 71.8]	
1	long stretcher	$^3/_4$ x $2^5/_8$ x $63^1/_4$	[19.1 x 66.7 x 1606.5]	$59^3/_4$ between tenons
2	stretchers	$^3/_4$ x $2^3/_8$ x $17^3/_4$	[19.1 x 60.3 x 450.8]	17 between tenons
2	stretchers	$^3/_4$ x $2^3/_8$ x $10^1/_4$	[19.1 x 60.3 x 260.4]	$7^3/_4$ between tenons
1	front apron	$^3/_4$ x $3^1/_4$ x $42^1/_{16}$	[19.1 x 82.5 x 1068.4]	add for tenons
2	angled panels	$^3/_4$ x 9 x 12	[19.1 x 228.6 x 304.8]	
2	side panels	$^3/_4$ x 9 x $8^1/_2$	[19.1 x 228.6 x 216]	$7^3/_4$ between tenons
1	back panel	$^3/_4$ x 9 x $60^1/_2$	[19.1 x 228.6 x 1536.7]	$59^3/_4$ between tenons
2	dividers	$^3/_4$ x $4^1/_4$ x $17^3/_4$	[19.1 x 108 x 450.8]	17 between tenons
1	dividers	$^3/_4$ x $4^1/_4$ x $18^1/_8$	[19.1 x 108 x 460.4]	$17^3/_8$ between tenons
1	drawer front divider	$^3/_4$ x $1^1/_4$ x $4^1/_4$	[19.1 x 31.8 x 108]	
2	drawer fronts	$^3/_4$ x $4^1/_4$ x $20^3/_8$	[19.1 x 108 x 517.5]	opening
1	rail above drawers	$^3/_4$ x $1^3/_8$ x $42^1/_{16}$	[19.1 x 34.9 x 1068.4]	add for tenons
4	side trim	$^1/_8$ x $^3/_4$ x $7^{13}/_{16}$	[3.2 x 19.1 x 198.4]	
4	angled trim	$^1/_8$ x $^3/_4$ x $12^{13}/_{16}$	[3.2 x 19.1 x 309.6]	
2	front trim	$^1/_8$ x $^3/_4$ x $42^1/_{16}$	[3.2 x 19.1 x 1068.4	

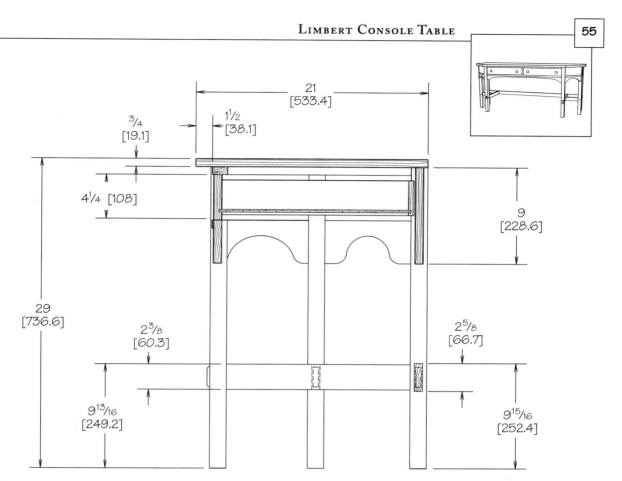

3/4
[19.1]

1 1/2
[38.1]

21
[533.4]

4 1/4 [108]

9
[228.6]

29
[736.6]

2 3/8
[60.3]

2 5/8
[66.7]

9 13/16
[249.2]

9 15/16
[252.4]

Side section

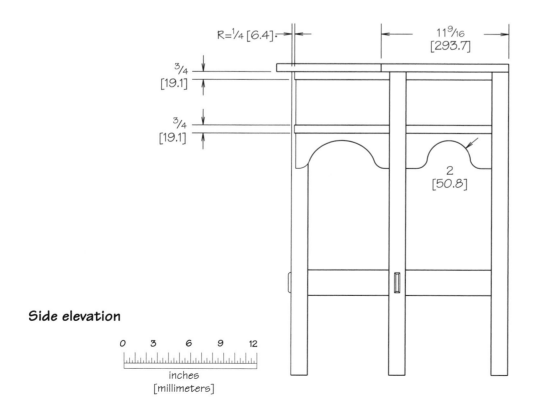

R=1/4 [6.4]

11 9/16
[293.7]

3/4
[19.1]

3/4
[19.1]

2
[50.8]

Side elevation

0   3   6   9   12

inches
[millimeters]

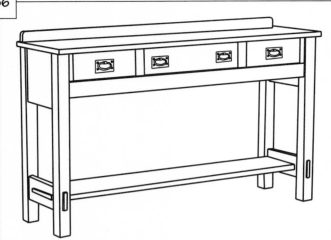

GUSTAV STICKLEY NO. 962 SERVER

36 high x 59 1/4 wide x 17 deep
[915 x 1505 x 432]

This design appeared in 1902, and could be considered the granddaddy of Gustav Stickley's servers. In later years many variations on this theme were produced, usually in smaller versions, without the exposed joinery this piece features.

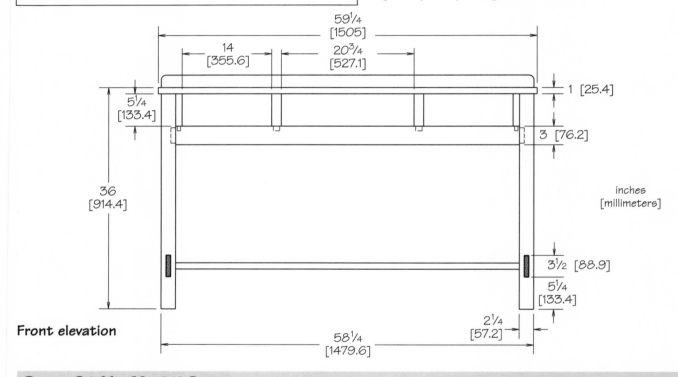

Front elevation

inches [millimeters]

Gustav Stickley No. 962 Server

QTY	PART	SIZE		NOTES
4	legs	$2^1/4$ x $2^1/4$ x 35	[57.2 x 57.2 x 889]	
2	rails	$1^1/4$ x $4^1/2$ x 17	[31.8 x 114.3 x 431.8]	12 [304.8] between tenons
1	lower shelf	1 x 11 x $57^1/2$	[25.4 x 279.4 x 1460.5]	55 [1397] between tenons
2	end panels	$3/4$ x $10^1/2$ x $13^1/2$	[19.1 x 266.7 x 342.9]	12 [304.8] between tenons
1	back panel	$3/4$ x $8^1/4$ x $54^1/2$	[19.1 x 209.6 x 1384.3]	$53^3/4$ [1365.3] between tenons
2	dividers between drawers	$3/4$ x $6^1/2$ x $14^3/4$	[19.1 x 165.1 x 374.7]	
1	front rail	$7/8$ x 3 x $55^3/4$	[22.2 x 76.2 x 1416.1]	$53^3/4$ [1365.3] between tenons
1	rail above drawers	$3/4$ x $1^1/2$ x $54^3/4$	[19.1 x 38.1 x 1390.7]	$53^3/4$ [1365.3] between tenons
2	vertical @ drawers	$3/4$ x 1 x 6	[19.1 x 25.4 x 152.4]	$5^1/4$ [133.4] exposed
2	vertical between drawers	$3/4$ x $1^1/2$ x 6	[19.1 x 38.1 x 152.4]	$5^1/4$ [133.4] exposed
2	drawer fronts	$3/4$ x $5^1/4$ x 14	[19.1 x 133.4 x 355.6]	opening
1	drawer front	$3/4$ x $5^1/4$ x $20^3/4$	[19.1 x 133.4 x 527.1]	opening
1	top	1 x 17 x $59^1/4$	[25.4 x 431.8 x 1505]	
1	backsplash	$7/8$ x 2 x $58^1/4$	[22.2 x 50.8 x 1479.6]	

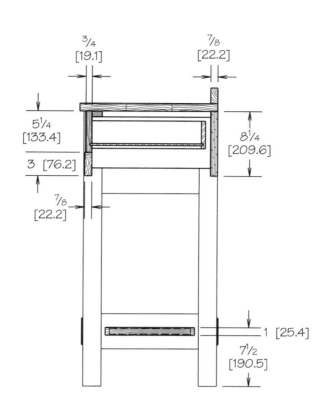

3/4
[19.1]

7/8
[22.2]

5 1/4
[133.4]

3 [76.2]

7/8
[22.2]

8 1/4
[209.6]

1 [25.4]

7 1/2
[190.5]

Side section

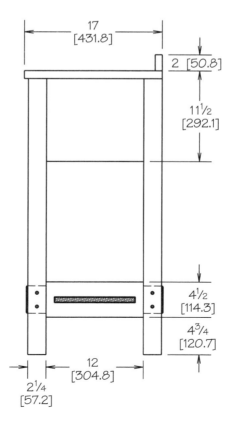

17
[431.8]

2 [50.8]

11 1/2
[292.1]

4 1/2
[114.3]

4 3/4
[120.7]

12
[304.8]

2 1/4
[57.2]

Side elevation

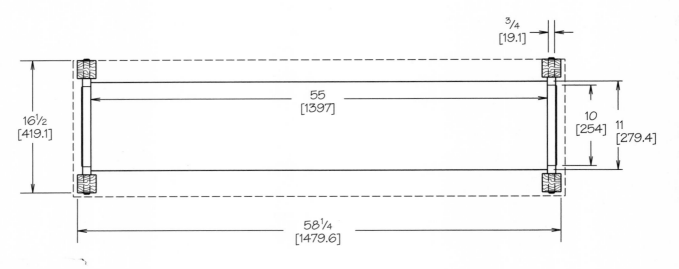

3/4
[19.1]

55
[1397]

16 1/2
[419.1]

10
[254]

11
[279.4]

58 1/4
[1479.6]

Plan section above shelf

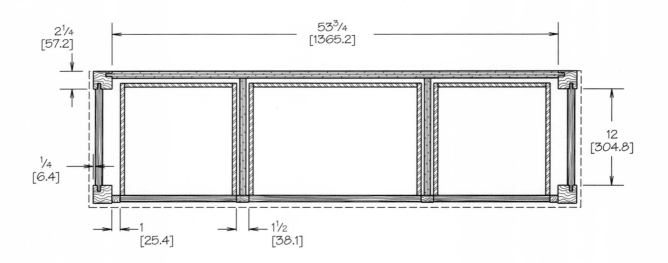

2 1/4
[57.2]

53 3/4
[1365.2]

12
[304.8]

1/4
[6.4]

1
[25.4]

1 1/2
[38.1]

Plan section through drawers

0 3 6 9 12

inches
[millimeters]

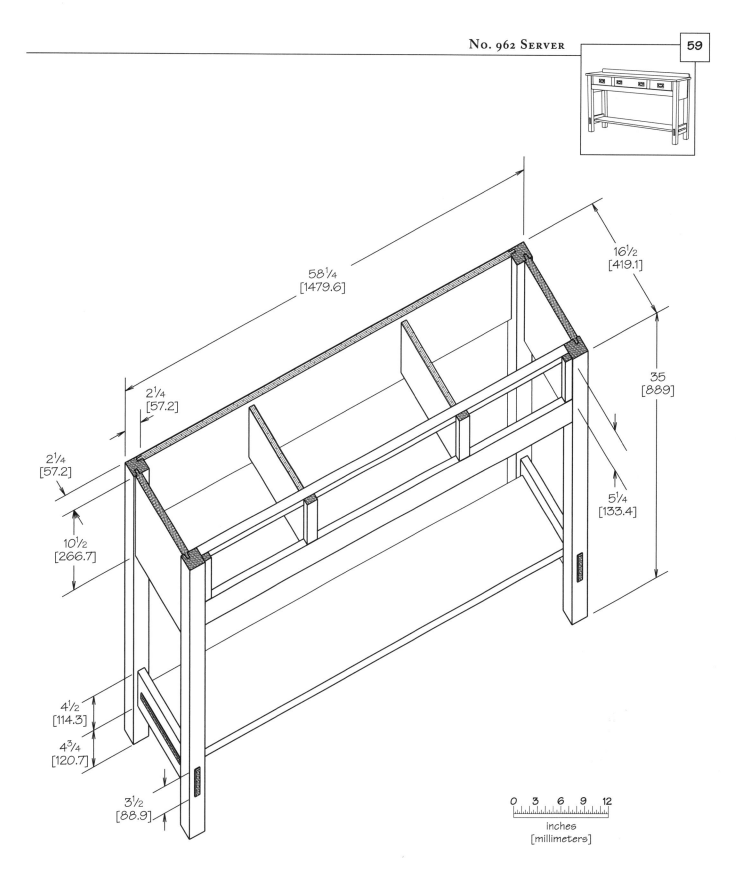

58¹⁄₄
[1479.6]

16¹⁄₂
[419.1]

2¹⁄₄
[57.2]

35
[889]

2¹⁄₄
[57.2]

5¹⁄₄
[133.4]

10¹⁄₂
[266.7]

4¹⁄₂
[114.3]

4³⁄₄
[120.7]

3¹⁄₂
[88.9]

0   3   6   9   12

inches
[millimeters]

Assembly

L. & J. G. STICKLEY
NO. 729 CHINA CABINET
70 high x 50 wide x 17 deep [1778 x 1270 x 432]

This very large cabinet could be put to a variety of contemporary uses. However if it was to house electronic gear, it might need to be made a few inches deeper. You'll have to shop around to find suitable hardware, though reproduction specialists generally do carry large strap hinges like the ones on the lower section.

L. & J. G. Stickley No. 729 China Cabinet

QTY	PART	SIZE		NOTES
2	sides	1 x 16$\frac{1}{8}$ x 69$\frac{1}{8}$	[25.4 x 409.6 x 1755.8]	assembled-parts detailed below
4	stiles	1 x 3$\frac{1}{4}$ x 69$\frac{1}{8}$	[25.4 x 82.6 x 1755.8]	
4	bottom & middle rails	1 x 5$\frac{1}{4}$ x 11$\frac{1}{8}$	[25.4 x 133.4 x 282.6]	9$\frac{5}{8}$ [244.5] between tenons
2	top rails	1 x 2$\frac{1}{4}$ x 11$\frac{1}{8}$	[25.4 x 57.2 x 282.6]	9$\frac{5}{8}$ [244.5] between tenons
2	mullions	1 x 1$\frac{1}{8}$ x 41$\frac{1}{4}$	[25.4 x 28.6 x 1047.8]	40$\frac{1}{4}$ [1022.4] between tenons
12	muntins	1 x 1$\frac{1}{8}$ x 5$\frac{1}{4}$	[25.4 x 28.6 x 133.4]	4$\frac{1}{4}$ [108] between tenons
2	upper doors	$\frac{7}{8}$ x 22 x 45$\frac{1}{4}$	[22.2 x 558.8 x 1149.4]	opening-parts detailed below
2	hinge stiles	$\frac{7}{8}$ x 2$\frac{3}{4}$ x 45$\frac{1}{4}$	[22.2 x 69.9 x 1149.4]	
2	latch stiles	$\frac{7}{8}$ x 2$\frac{1}{4}$ x 45$\frac{1}{4}$	[22.2 x 57.2 x 1149.4	
2	bottom rails	$\frac{7}{8}$ x 2$\frac{3}{4}$ x 18$\frac{1}{2}$	[22.2 x 69.9 x 469.9]	17 [431.8] between tenons
2	top rails	$\frac{7}{8}$ x 2$\frac{1}{4}$ x 18$\frac{1}{2}$	[22.2 x 57.2 x 469.9]	17 [431.8] between tenons
4	mullions	$\frac{7}{8}$ x 1$\frac{1}{8}$ x 41$\frac{3}{4}$	[22.2 x 28.6 x 1060.5]	40$\frac{1}{4}$ [1022.4] between tenons
18	muntins	$\frac{7}{8}$ x 1$\frac{1}{8}$ x 5$\frac{11}{16}$	[22.2 x 28.6 x 144.5]	4$\frac{15}{16}$ [125.4] between tenons
2	lower doors	$\frac{7}{8}$ x 22 x 17$\frac{5}{8}$	[22.2 x 558.8 x 447.7]	opening
1	bottom	1 x 16 x 45$\frac{3}{4}$	[25.4 x 406.4 x 1162.1]	45 [1143] between tenons
1	fixed shelf	1 x 15$\frac{1}{4}$ x 45$\frac{3}{4}$	[25.4 x 387.4 x 1162.1]	45 [1143] between tenons
1	top	$\frac{7}{8}$ x 17 x 50	[22.2 x 431.8 x 1270]	
1	lower vertical divider	1 x 15$\frac{1}{4}$ x 18$\frac{3}{8}$	[25.4 x 387.4 x 466.7]	17$\frac{5}{8}$ [447.7] between tenons
2	lower doorstops	$\frac{3}{4}$ x $\frac{3}{4}$ x 17$\frac{5}{8}$	[19.1 x 19.1 x 447.7]	
1	upper divider stile	1 x 1$\frac{3}{4}$ x 45$\frac{1}{4}$	[25.4 x 44.5 x 1149.4]	
2	upper door stops	$\frac{3}{4}$ x $\frac{3}{4}$ x 45$\frac{1}{4}$	[19.1 x 19.1 x 1149.4]	
3	upper shelves	$\frac{3}{4}$ x 13$\frac{3}{8}$ x 45	[19.1 x 339.7 x 1143]	
2	lower shelves	$\frac{3}{4}$ x 13$\frac{3}{8}$ x 22	[19.1 x 339.7 x 558.8]	
1	arched apron	$\frac{3}{4}$ x 2$\frac{1}{4}$ x 45$\frac{3}{4}$	[19.1 x 57.2 x 1162.1]	45 [1143] between tenons
8	back planks	$\frac{3}{4}$ x 5$\frac{3}{4}$ x 64$\frac{3}{8}$	[19.1 x 146.1 x 1635.1]	

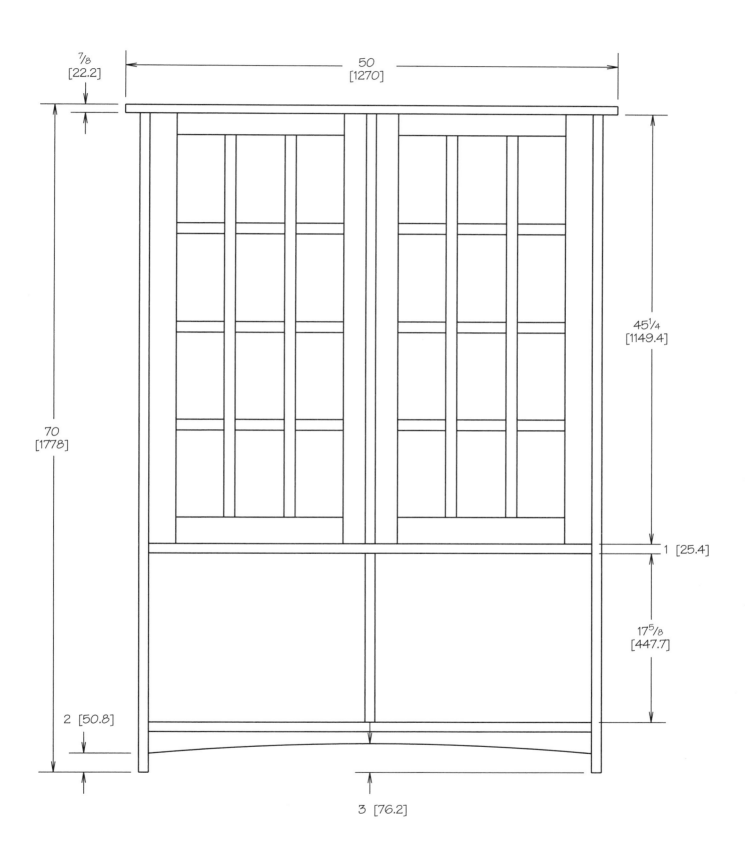

Front elevation

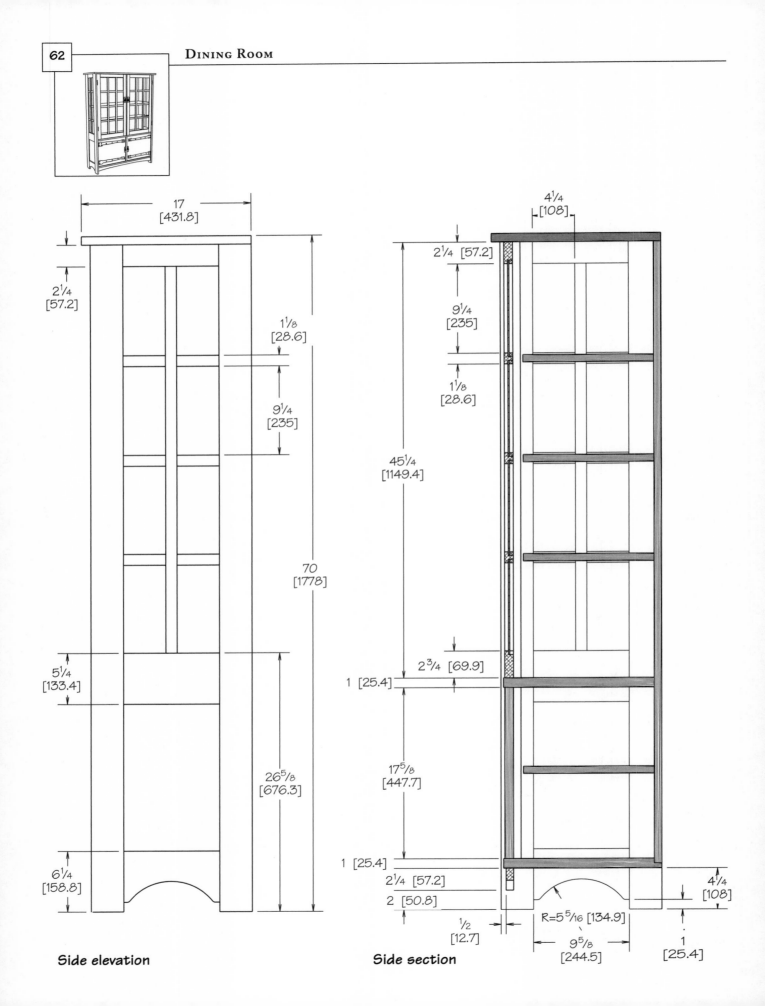

17
[431.8]

$2^{1}/_{4}$
[57.2]

$1^{1}/_{8}$
[28.6]

$9^{1}/_{4}$
[235]

70
[1778]

$5^{1}/_{4}$
[133.4]

$26^{5}/_{8}$
[676.3]

$6^{1}/_{4}$
[158.8]

$4^{1}/_{4}$
[108]

$2^{1}/_{4}$ [57.2]

$9^{1}/_{4}$
[235]

$1^{1}/_{8}$
[28.6]

$45^{1}/_{4}$
[1149.4]

$2^{3}/_{4}$ [69.9]

1 [25.4]

$17^{5}/_{8}$
[447.7]

1 [25.4]

$2^{1}/_{4}$ [57.2]

2 [50.8]

$^{1}/_{2}$
[12.7]

R=$5^{5}/_{16}$ [134.9]

$9^{5}/_{8}$
[244.5]

$4^{1}/_{4}$
[108]

1
[25.4]

Side elevation

Side section

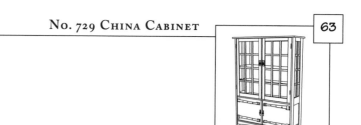

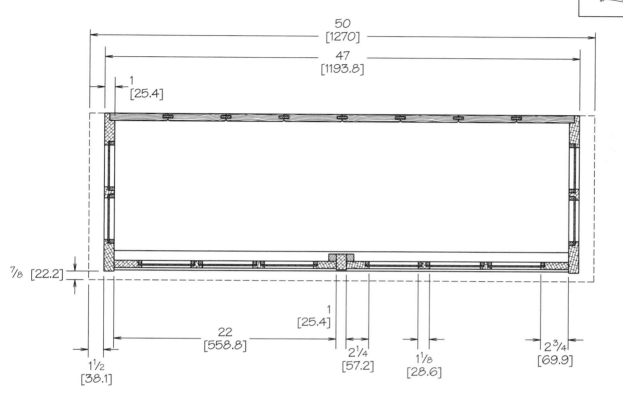

50
[1270]

47
[1193.8]

1
[25.4]

7/8 [22.2]

1
[25.4]

22
[558.8]

2 1/4
[57.2]

1 1/8
[28.6]

2 3/4
[69.9]

1 1/2
[38.1]

Plan section through top

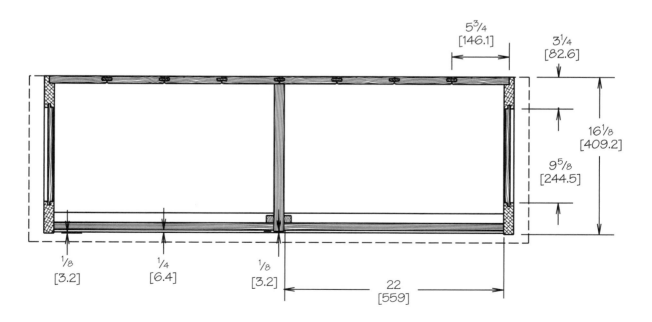

5 3/4
[146.1]

3 1/4
[82.6]

16 1/8
[409.2]

9 5/8
[244.5]

1/8
[3.2]

1/4
[6.4]

1/8
[3.2]

22
[559]

Plan section through base

GUSTAV STICKLEY
NO. 803 CHINA CABINET

60 high x 36 wide x 15 deep [1524 x 914 x 381]

A classic example of the high points of Harvey Ellis' designs—a thin top with a wide overhang, arches at the top of the door and the bottom front rail, and subtly tapered legs.

The legs actually have a flat area between the two tapers—see the front section.

Make the door well, and use good hinges.

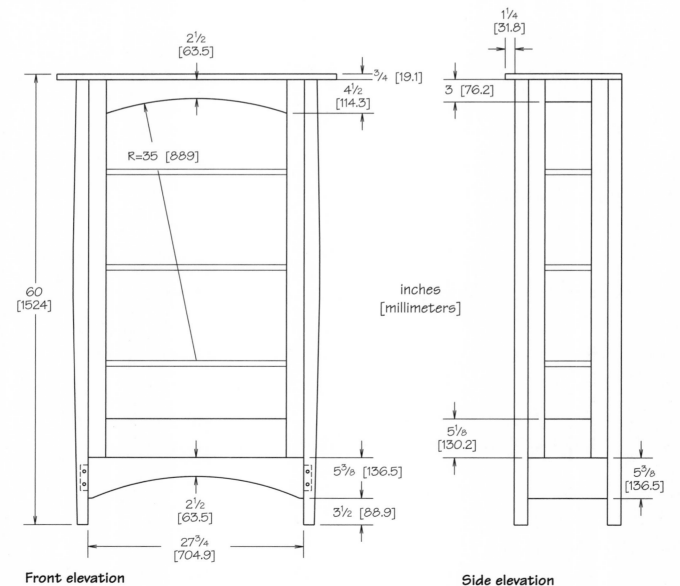

$2\frac{1}{2}$ [63.5]

$\frac{3}{4}$ [19.1]

$4\frac{1}{2}$ [114.3]

R=35 [889]

60 [1524]

inches [millimeters]

$5\frac{3}{8}$ [136.5]

$2\frac{1}{2}$ [63.5]

$3\frac{1}{2}$ [88.9]

$27\frac{3}{4}$ [704.9]

$1\frac{1}{4}$ [31.8]

3 [76.2]

$5\frac{1}{8}$ [130.2]

$5\frac{3}{8}$ [136.5]

Front elevation

Side elevation

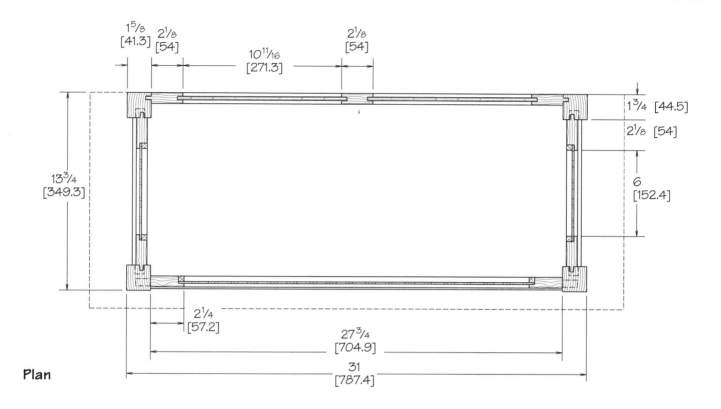

Plan

Gustav Stickley No. 803 China Cabinet

QTY	PART	SIZE		NOTES
4	legs	1³⁄₄ x 2 x 59¹⁄₄	[44.5 x 50.8 x 1505]	
1	door	³⁄₄ x 27³⁄₄ x 50	[19.1 x 704.9 x 1270]	opening-parts detailed below
2	stiles	³⁄₄ x 2¹⁄₄ x 50	[19.1 x 57.2 x1270]	
1	top rail	³⁄₄ x 4¹⁄₂ x 25¹⁄₄	[19.1 x 114.3 x 641.4]	23¹⁄₄ [590.6] between tenons
1	bottom rail	³⁄₄ x 5¹⁄₂ x 25¹⁄₄	[19.1 x 139.7 x 641.4]	23¹⁄₄ [590.6] between tenons
1	arched apron	⁷⁄₈ x 5³⁄₈ x 29¹⁄₂	[22.2 x 136.5 x 749.3]	27³⁄₄ [704.9] between tenons
2	side panels	³⁄₄ x 10¹⁄₄ x 50³⁄₈	[19.1 x 260.4 x 1279.5]	assembled — parts detailed below
4	stiles	³⁄₄ x 2¹⁄₂ x 50³⁄₈	[19.1 x 63.5 x 1279.5]	2¹⁄₈ [54] exposed
2	bottom rails	³⁄₄ x 5¹⁄₂ x 6³⁄₄	[19.1 x 139.7 x 171.5]	5¹⁄₈ x 6 [130.2 x 152.4] between tenons
2	top rails	³⁄₄ x 3 x 6³⁄₄	[19.1 x 76.2 x 171.5]	6 [152.4] between tenons
2	lower rails	⁷⁄₈ x 5³⁄₈ x 11¹⁄₂	[22.2 x 136.5 x 292.1]	10¹⁄₄ [260.4] between tenons
1	back panel	³⁄₄ x 28¹⁄₂ x 50³⁄₈	[19.1 x 723.9 x 1279.5]	assembled—27³⁄₄ x 50 [704.9 x 1270] exposed-parts detailed below
2	outer stiles	³⁄₄ x 2¹⁄₂ x 50³⁄₈	[19.1 x 63.5 x 1279.5]	2¹⁄₈ [54] exposed
1	mid stile	³⁄₄ x 2¹⁄₈ x 43	[19.1 x 54 x 1092.2]	42¹⁄₄ [1073.2] between tenons
1	bottom rail	³⁄₄ x 5¹⁄₂ x 23¹⁄₂	[19.1 x 139.7 x 596.9]	22³⁄₄ [577.9] between tenons
1	top rail	³⁄₄ x 3 x 23¹⁄₂	[19.1 x 76.2 x 596.9]	22³⁄₄ [577.9] between tenons
2	panels	¹⁄₄ x 11⁷⁄₁₆ x 43	[6.4 x 290.5 x 1092.2]	42¹⁄₄ [1073.2] between tenons
1	bottom arched apron	³⁄₄ x 4⁵⁄₈ x 29¹⁄₂	[19.1 x 117.5 x 749.3]	27³⁄₄ [704.9] between tenons
1	bottom	³⁄₄ x 12³⁄₄ x 28¹⁄₄	[19.1 x 323.9 x 717.6]	
3	shelves	³⁄₄ x 11⁷⁄₈ x 28¹⁄₄	[19.1 x 301.6 x 717.6]	notch corners at legs
1	top	³⁄₄ x 15 x 36	[19.1 x 381 x 914.4]	

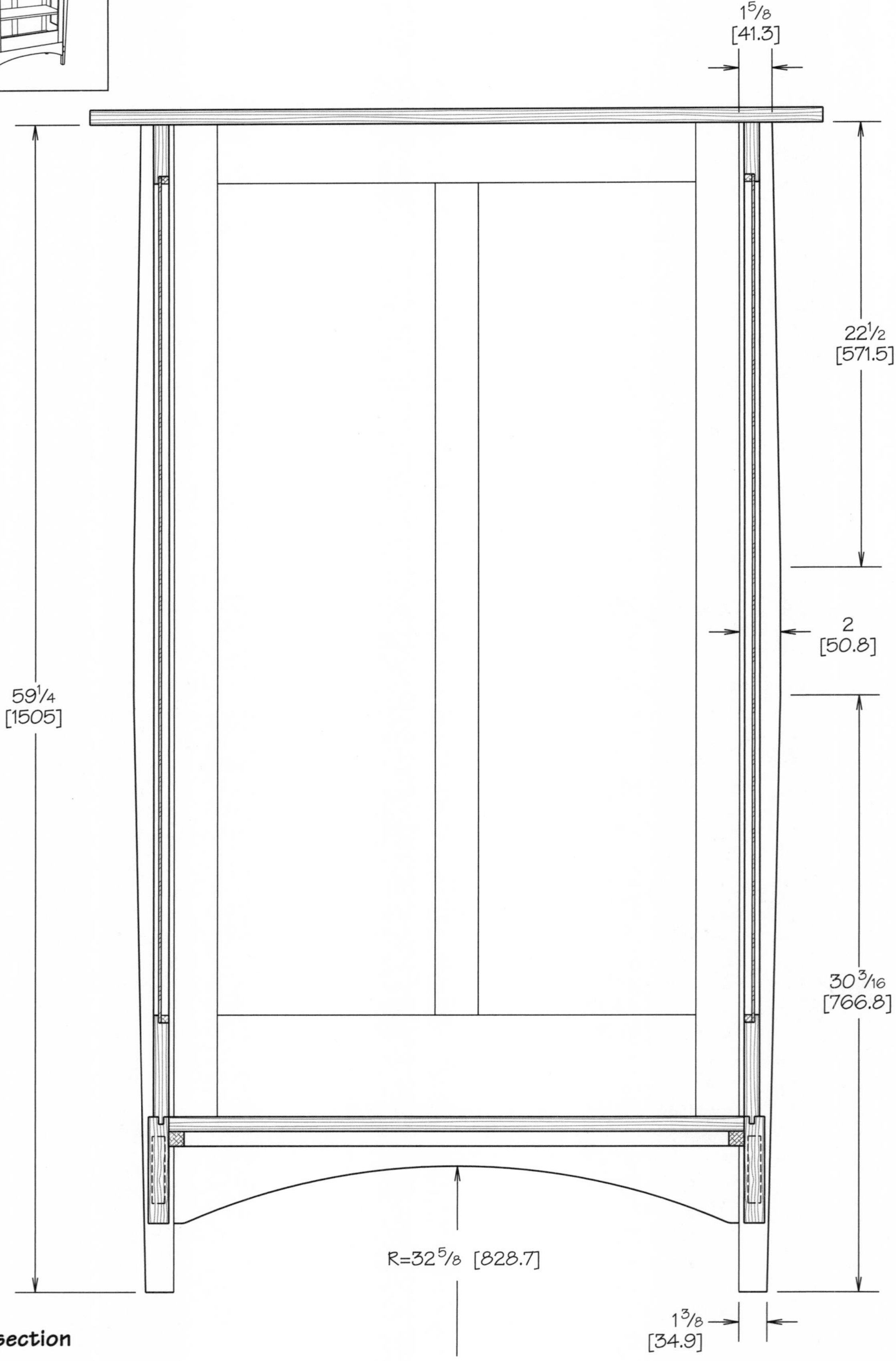

1⁵⁄₈
[41.3]

22¹⁄₂
[571.5]

2
[50.8]

59¹⁄₄
[1505]

30³⁄₁₆
[766.8]

R=32⁵⁄₈ [828.7]

1³⁄₈
[34.9]

Front section

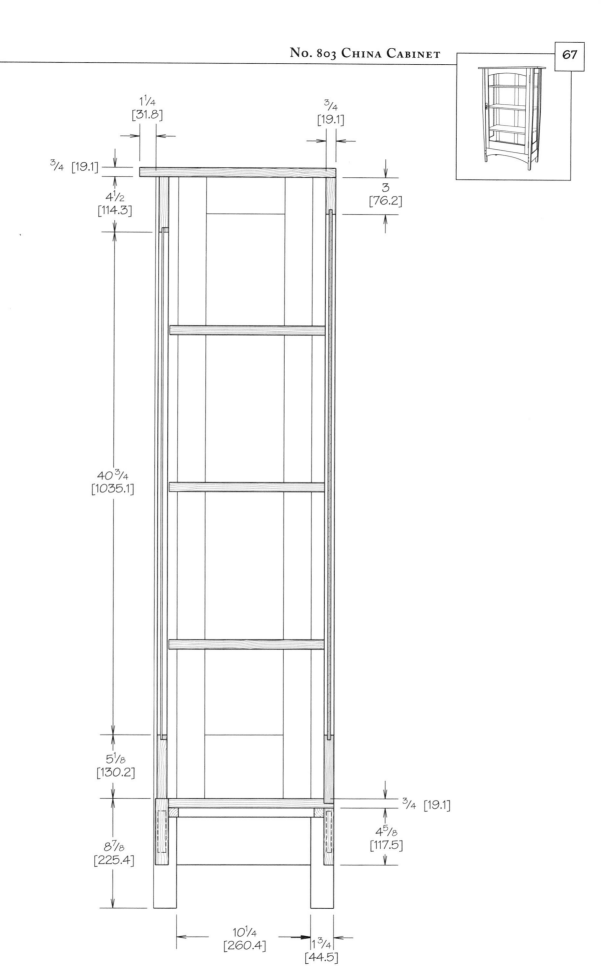

1¼
[31.8]

¾
[19.1]

¾ [19.1]

3
[76.2]

4½
[114.3]

40¾
[1035.1]

5⅛
[130.2]

¾ [19.1]

4⅝
[117.5]

8⅞
[225.4]

10¼
[260.4]

1¾
[44.5]

Side section

GUSTAV STICKLEY
NO. 66 WALL MIRROR

36 wide x 28 high [914 x 711]

I was surprised to see the piece of plywood on the back of the original, but it makes sense—it stiffens and strengthens the frame. If you use 1/4" thick mirror as drawn, it will be heavy. In some catalog illustrations, mirrors like this were shown with three or four coat hooks attached to the bottom rail.

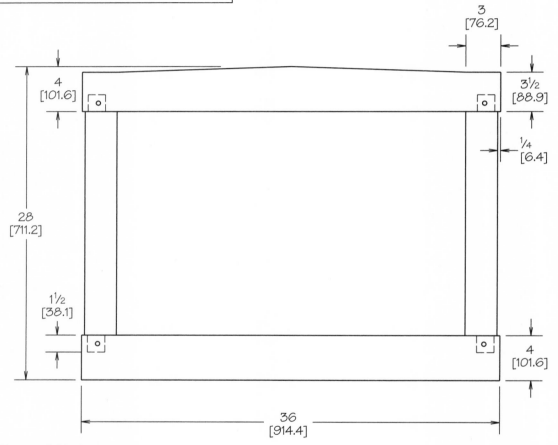

Front elevation

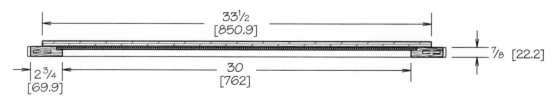

Plan section

0 3 6 9 12

inches
[millimeters]

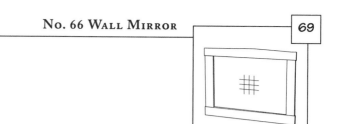

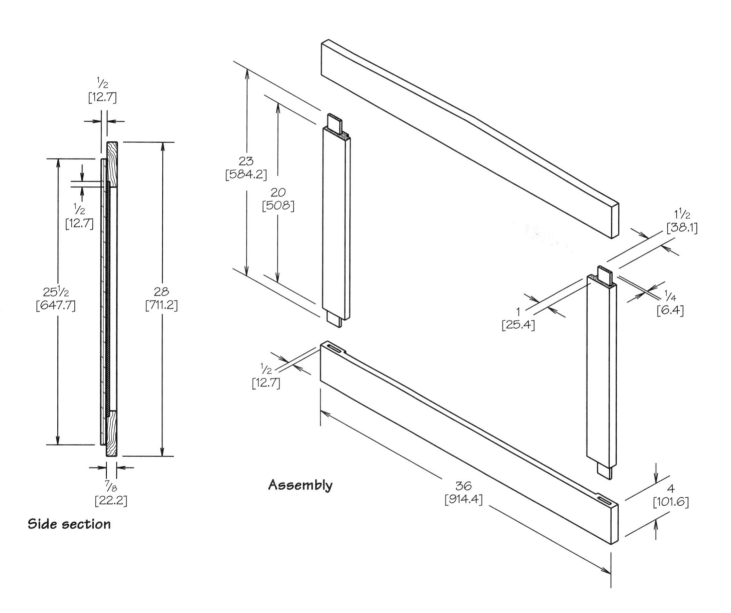

Side section

Assembly

Gustav Stickley No. 66 Wall Mirror

QTY	PART	SIZE		NOTES
2	stiles	⁷/₈ x 3 x 23	[22.2 x 76.2 x 584.2]	20 [508] between tenons
1	bottom rail	⁷/₈ x 4 x 36	[22.2 x 101.6 x 914.4]	
1	top rail	⁷/₈ x 4 x 36	[22.2 x 101.6 x 914.4]	tapers to 3¹/₂ [88.9] at ends
1	back	¹/₂ x 25¹/₂ x 33¹/₂	[12.7 x 647.7 x 850.9]	plywood

LIVING ROOM

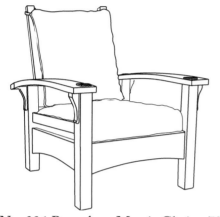

No. 336 Bow-Arm Morris Chair   72

No. 323 Rocker   76

No. 1292 Footstool   85

No. 347 Eastwood Easy Chair   80

No. 206 Love Seat Settle 88

No. 225 Small Settle 92

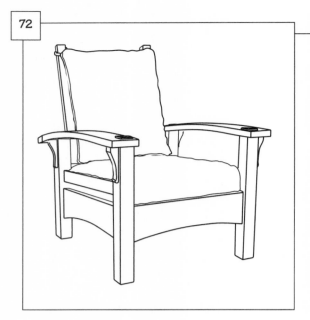

GUSTAV STICKLEY
NO. 336 BOW ARM MORRIS CHAIR
31½ wide x 37 high x 37 deep [800 x 940 x 940]

Although this looks like it could be a Harvey Ellis design, this chair originally appeared, with slightly different legs, in 1901, two years before Ellis came to work for Stickley. The loose seat cushion was used until 1909, when it was replaced with a spring cushion. The steam-bent bowed arms, plus the angle of the cushion, make this one of the most comfortable of all the Morris chairs. Later versions of this chair had legs that were 2 inches longer, added to the bottom of the leg, as seen in the perspective view at left.

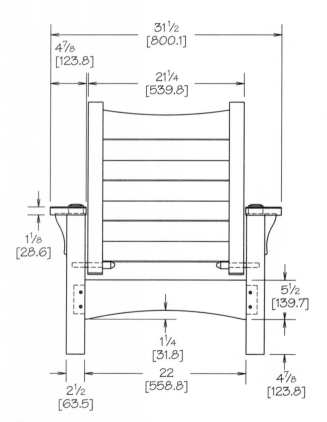

Front elevation

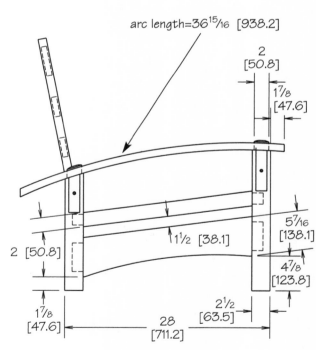

Side elevation

arc length=36¹⁵⁄₁₆ [938.2]

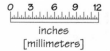

0 3 6 9 12

inches
[millimeters]

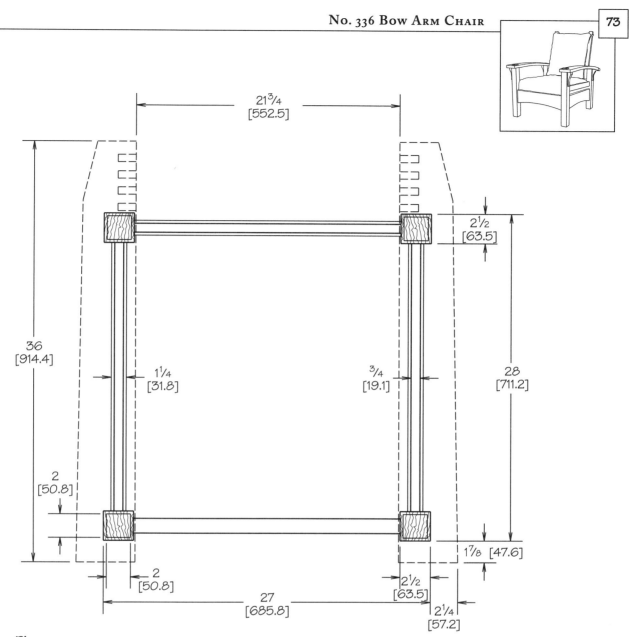

Plan

Gustav Stickley No. 336 Bow Arm Morris Chair

Qty	Part	Size		Notes
2	front legs	$2^1/2$ x $2^1/2$ x $21^1/16$	[63.5 x 63.5 x 535]	$19^5/8$ [498.5] to high point below arm
2	rear legs	$2^1/2$ x $2^1/2$ x $17^9/16$	[63.5 x 63.5 x 446.1]	$16^3/8$ [415.9] to high point below arm
1	front rail	$1^1/4$ x $5^1/2$ x 25	[31.8 x 139.7 x 635]	22 [558.8] between tenons
1	lower back rail	$1^1/4$ x $5^1/2$ x 25	[31.8 x 139.7 x 635]	22 [558.8] between tenons
1	upper back rail	$3/4$ x 2 x 25	[19.1 x 50.8 x 635]	22 [558.8] between tenons
2	lower side rails	$1^1/4$ x $5^7/16$ x 26	[31.8 x 138.1 x 660.4]	23 [584.2] between angled tenons
2	upper side rails	$3/4$ x 2 x 26	[19.1 x 50.8 x 660.4]	23 [584.2] between angled tenons
2	arms	$1^1/8$ x $4^7/8$ x $36^{15}/16$	[28.6 x 123.8 x 938.2]	finished arc length
4	corbels	$1^1/2$ x $1^9/16$ x $5^7/8$	[38.1 x 39.7 x 149.2]	
2	back uprights	$1^1/8$ x 2 x $24^3/4$	[28.6 x 50.8 x 628.7]	
3	curved back rails	$3/4$ x $2^3/4$ x $19^1/4$	[19.1 x 69.9 x 489]	$17^1/4$ [438.2] between tenons-make longer for bending
1	back top rail	$3/4$ x $4^1/4$ x $19^1/4$	[19.1 x 108 x 489]	$17^1/4$ [438.2] between tenons-make longer for bending

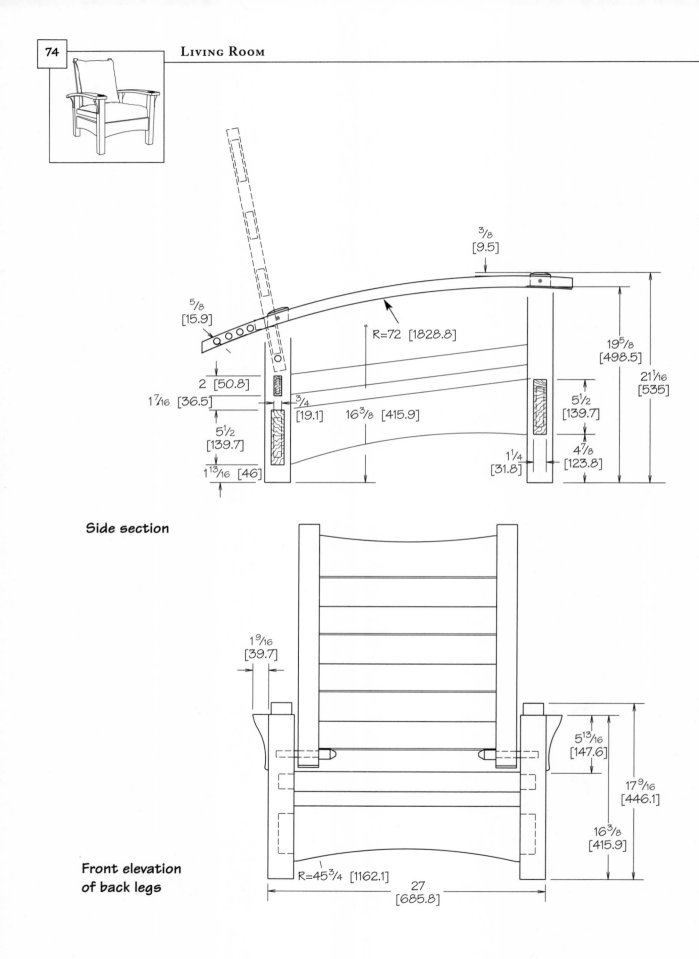

3/8
[9.5]

5/8
[15.9]

R=72 [1828.8]

19 5/8
[498.5]

21 1/16
[535]

2 [50.8]

1 7/16 [36.5]

3/4
[19.1]

16 3/8 [415.9]

5 1/2
[139.7]

5 1/2
[139.7]

1 1/4
[31.8]

4 7/8
[123.8]

1 13/16 [46]

Side section

1 9/16
[39.7]

5 13/16
[147.6]

17 9/16
[446.1]

16 3/8
[415.9]

**Front elevation
of back legs**

R=45 3/4 [1162.1]

27
[685.8]

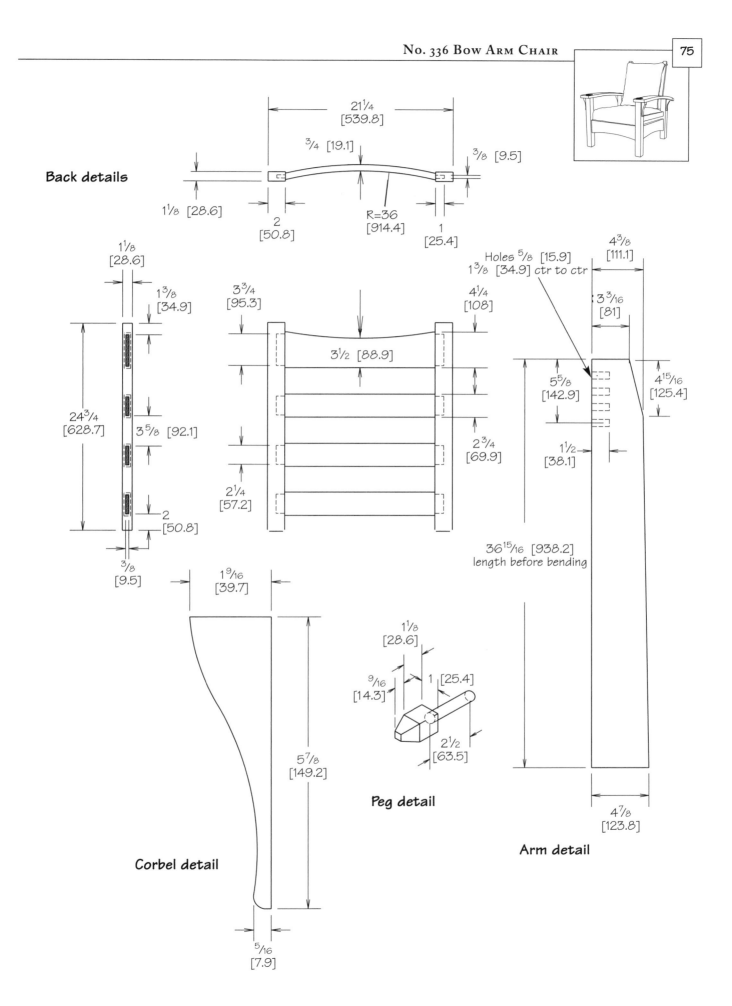

Back details

21¼ [539.8]

¾ [19.1]

⅜ [9.5]

1⅛ [28.6]

2 [50.8]

R=36 [914.4]

1 [25.4]

1⅛ [28.6]

1⅜ [34.9]

24¾ [628.7]

3⅝ [92.1]

2 [50.8]

⅜ [9.5]

3¾ [95.3]

3½ [88.9]

2¼ [57.2]

4¼ [108]

2¾ [69.9]

Holes ⅝ [15.9]
1⅜ [34.9] ctr to ctr

4⅜ [111.1]

3³⁄₁₆ [81]

5⅝ [142.9]

4¹⁵⁄₁₆ [125.4]

1½ [38.1]

36¹⁵⁄₁₆ [938.2]
length before bending

1⁹⁄₁₆ [39.7]

5⅞ [149.2]

1⅛ [28.6]

⁹⁄₁₆ [14.3]

1 [25.4]

2½ [63.5]

Peg detail

4⅞ [123.8]

Arm detail

Corbel detail

⁵⁄₁₆ [7.9]

GUSTAV STICKLEY NO. 323 ROCKER
40 high x 30 wide x 30 deep (1016 x 762 x 762]

The original of this chair had a drop-in spring seat cushion, covered in leather. There was also a back cushion that tied to the top of the back posts. A note about the drawing views—the plan, front elevation, elevation of the back, and side section are all drawn with the arms and side rails parallel to the plane of the floor. Technically this is not correct, but it shows the important parts in their true sizes and shapes. Sometimes being incorrect is the right thing to do.

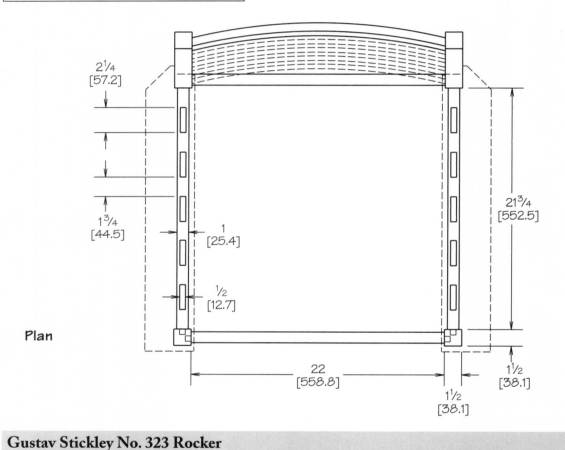

Plan

Gustav Stickley No. 323 Rocker

QTY	PART	SIZE		NOTES
2	front legs	$1^{1}/_{2}$ x $1^{1}/_{2}$ x $21^{1}/_{4}$	[38.1 x 38.1 x 539.8]	
2	back legs	$1^{1}/_{2}$ x $5^{7}/_{16}$ x 39	[38.1 x 138.1 x 990.6]	
2	rockers	$^{7}/_{8}$ x 2 x $32^{11}/_{16}$	[22.2 x 50.8 x 830.3]	arc length-make longer for bending
1	front rail	1 x $6^{1}/_{4}$ x 23	[25.4 x 158.8 x 584.2]	22 [558.8] between tenons
1	bottom back rail	1 x $6^{1}/_{4}$ x 23	[25.4 x 158.8 x 584.2]	22 [558.8] between tenons
5	curved back slats	$^{3}/_{4}$ x 3 x $24^{1}/_{4}$	[19.1 x 76.2 x 616]	22 [558.8] between tenons-make longer for bending
2	arms	$^{7}/_{8}$ x $4^{1}/_{4}$ x $25^{3}/_{4}$	[22.2 x 108 x 654.1]	
10	arm slats	$^{1}/_{2}$ x $2^{1}/_{4}$ x 12	[12.7 x 57.2 x 304.8]	$11^{1}/_{4}$ [285.8] between tenons
2	bottom side rails	1 x $6^{1}/_{4}$ x $23^{1}/_{4}$	[25.4 x 158.8 x 590.6]	$21^{3}/_{4}$ [552.5] between tenons
2	corbels	$^{3}/_{4}$ x $2^{1}/_{4}$ x 4	[19.1 x 57.2 x 101.6]	

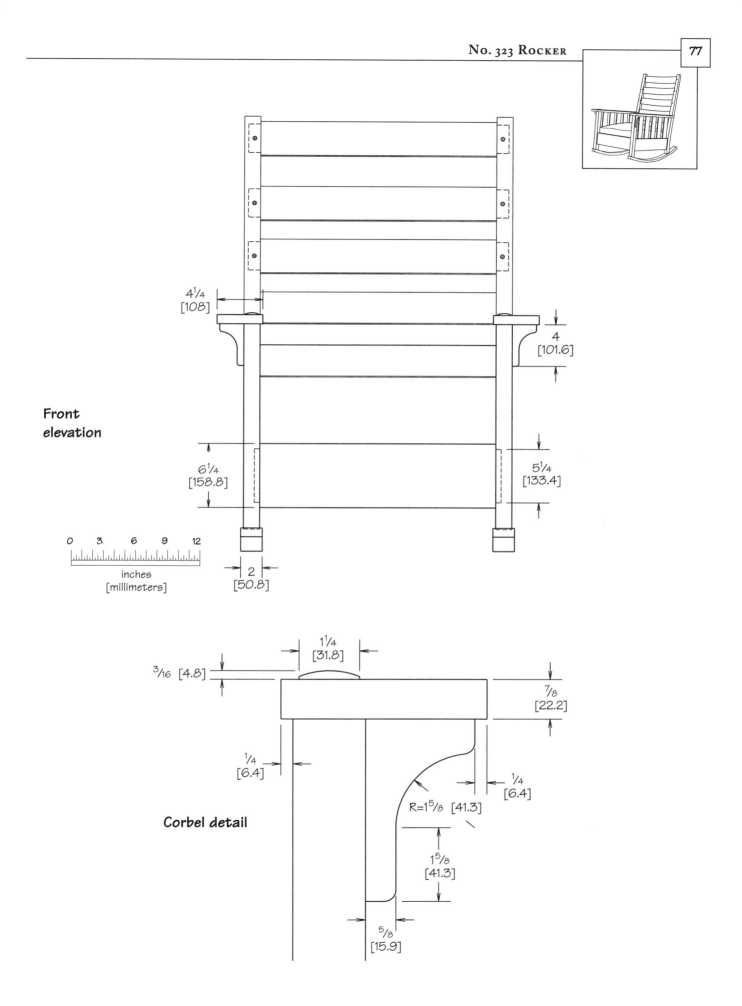

Front elevation

4¼
[108]

4
[101.6]

6¼
[158.8]

5¼
[133.4]

0   3   6   9   12

inches
[millimeters]

2
[50.8]

1¼
[31.8]

³⁄₁₆ [4.8]

⁷⁄₈
[22.2]

¼
[6.4]

¼
[6.4]

R=1⁵⁄₈ [41.3]

Corbel detail

1⁵⁄₈
[41.3]

⁵⁄₈
[15.9]

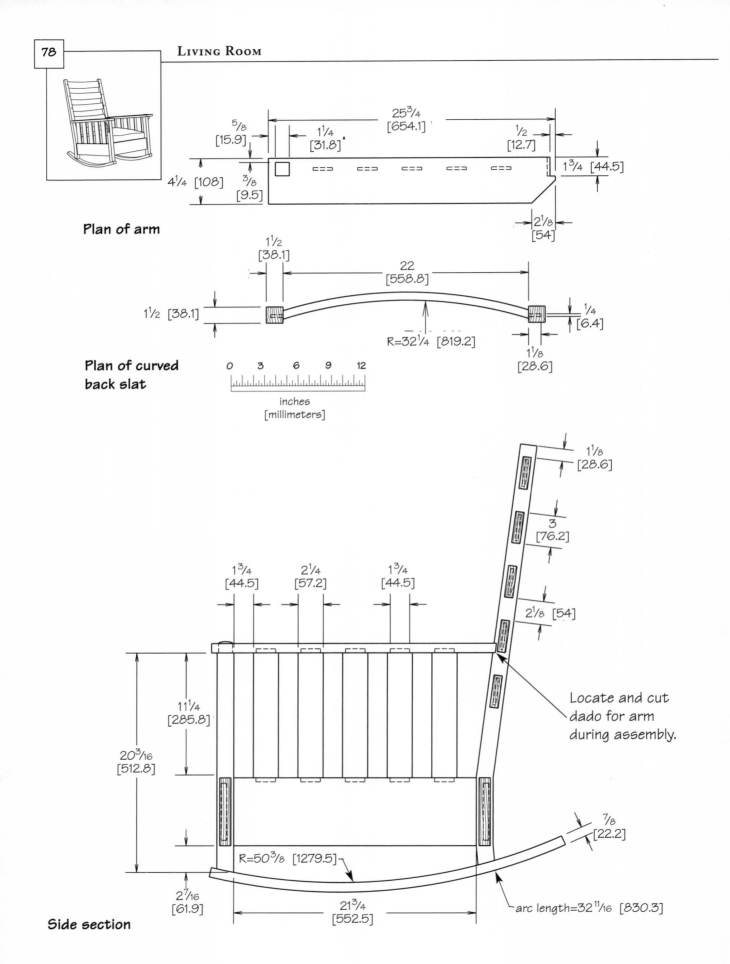

Plan of arm

5/8 [15.9]

1 1/4 [31.8]

25 3/4 [654.1]

1/2 [12.7]

1 3/4 [44.5]

4 1/4 [108]

3/8 [9.5]

2 1/8 [54]

Plan of curved back slat

1 1/2 [38.1]

22 [558.8]

1 1/2 [38.1]

R=32 1/4 [819.2]

1/4 [6.4]

1 1/8 [28.6]

0 3 6 9 12

inches [millimeters]

1 1/8 [28.6]

3 [76.2]

2 1/8 [54]

1 3/4 [44.5]

2 1/4 [57.2]

1 3/4 [44.5]

Locate and cut dado for arm during assembly.

11 1/4 [285.8]

20 3/16 [512.8]

7/8 [22.2]

R=50 3/8 [1279.5]

2 7/16 [61.9]

21 3/4 [552.5]

arc length=32 11/16 [830.3]

Side section

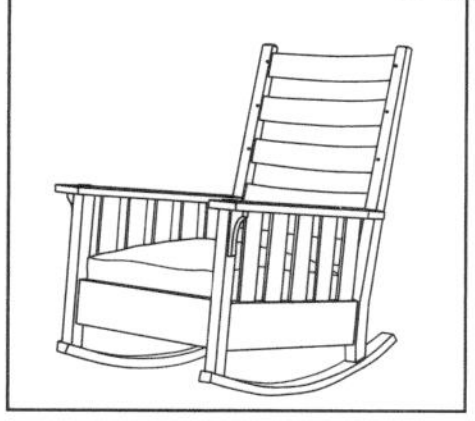

Elevation of back

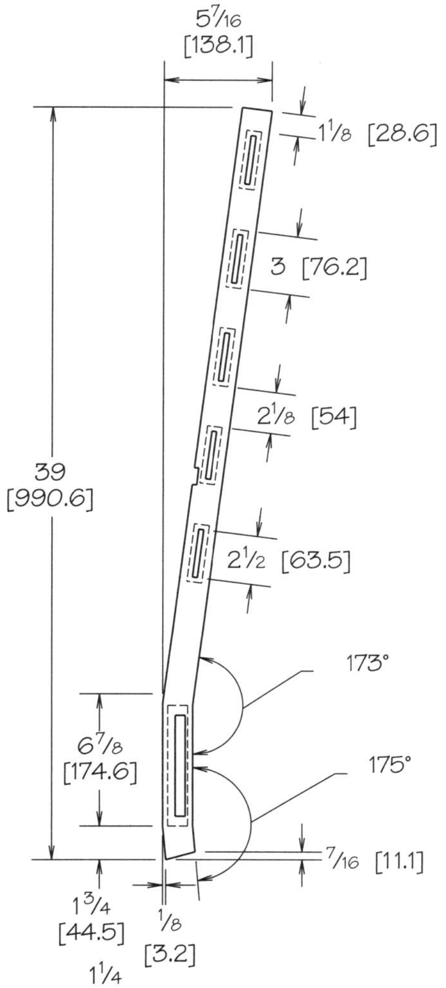
5⁷⁄16 [138.1]
1¹⁄8 [28.6]
3 [76.2]
2¹⁄8 [54]
39 [990.6]
2¹⁄2 [63.5]
173°
6⁷⁄8 [174.6]
175°
⁷⁄16 [11.1]
1³⁄4 [44.5]
¹⁄8 [3.2]

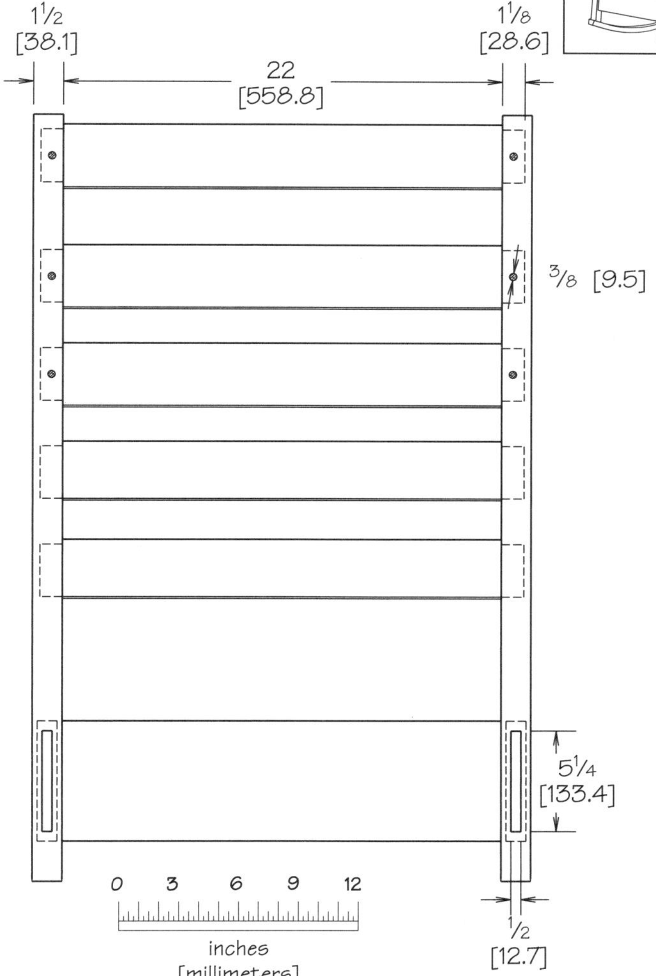
1¹⁄2 [38.1]
1¹⁄8 [28.6]
22 [558.8]
³⁄8 [9.5]
5¹⁄4 [133.4]
0 3 6 9 12
inches [millimeters]
¹⁄2 [12.7]

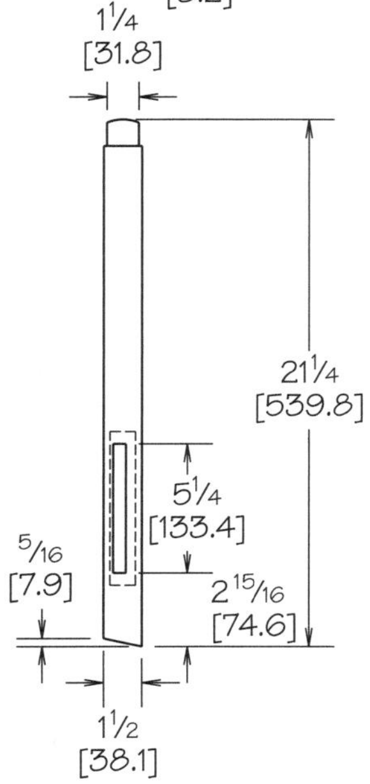
1¹⁄4 [31.8]
21¹⁄4 [539.8]
5¹⁄4 [133.4]
⁵⁄16 [7.9]
2¹⁵⁄16 [74.6]
1¹⁄2 [38.1]

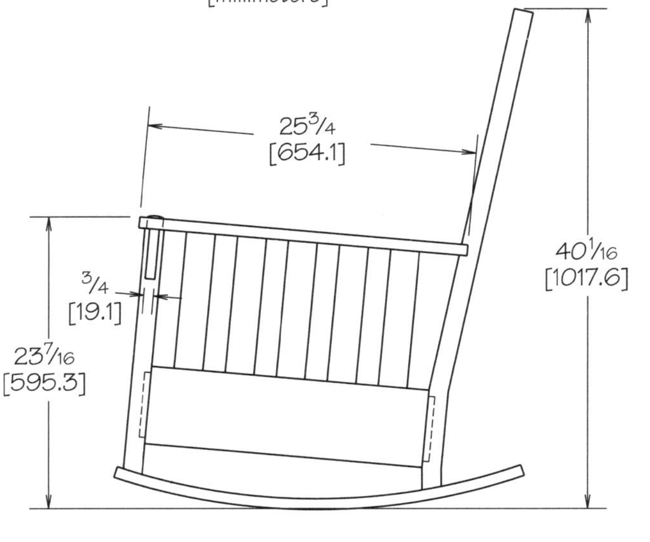
25³⁄4 [654.1]
³⁄4 [19.1]
23⁷⁄16 [595.3]
40¹⁄16 [1017.6]

Side elevation

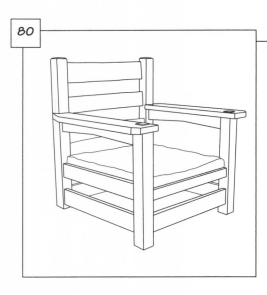

GUSTAV STICKLEY
NO. 347 EASTWOOD CHAIR

37 high x 38½ wide x 32½ deep [940 x 978 x 826]

Named after the suburb of Syracuse, New York, where Stickley's factory was located, this early chair was featured in "The Craftsman" Magazine in November 1901. A loose seat cushion was supported by a frame of woven cane supported inside the rails. I would run a 3/4" x 3/4" cleat inside the front and back seat rails, and support the cushion with thin wood slats. If you have the space for it, you won't find a more comfortable chair.

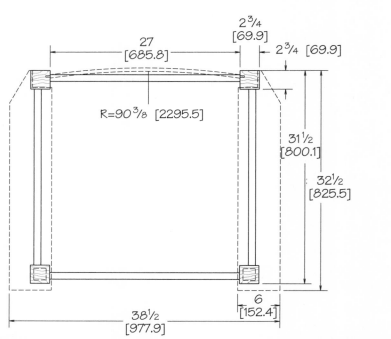

Plan

inches
[millimeters]

Gustav Stickley No. 347 Eastwood Chair

QTY	PART	SIZE		NOTES
2	front legs	2¾ x 2¾ x 23¹³/₁₆	[69.9 x 69.9 x 604.8]	22⁹/₁₆ [573.1] to top of shoulders below arms
2	back legs	2¾ x 2¾ x 38	[69.9 x 69.9 x 965.2]	
2	lower front & back rails	1 x 3¾ x 30	[25.4 x 95.3 x 762]	27 [685.8] between tenons
1	upper front rail	¾ x 2¼ x 30	[19.1 x 57.2 x 762]	27 [685.8] between tenons
1	upper back rail	¾ x 3¼ x 30	[19.1 x 82.6 x 762]	27 [685.8] between tenons
2	lower side rails	1 x 3¾ x 27⁹/₁₆	[25.4 x 95.3 x 700.1]	26 [660.4] between angled tenons
2	upper side rails	1 x 3¼ x 27⁹/₁₆	[25.4 x 82.6 x 700.1]	26 [660.4] between angled tenons
2	rails below arms	¾ x 3³/₁₆ x 27⁹/₁₆	[19.1 x 81 x 700.1]	26 [660.4] between angled tenons
1	top curved back rail	½ x 5 x 28¼	[12.7 x 127 x 717.6]	27 [685.8] between tenons-make longer for bending
1	middle curved back rail	½ x 4¼ x 28¼	[12.7 x 108 x 717.6]	27 [685.8] between tenons-make longer for bending
1	bottom curved back rail	½ x 3½ x 28¼	[12.7 x 88.9 x 717.6]	27 [685.8] between tenons-make longer for bending
2	arms	1 x 6 x 32½	[25.4 x 152.4 x 825.5]	

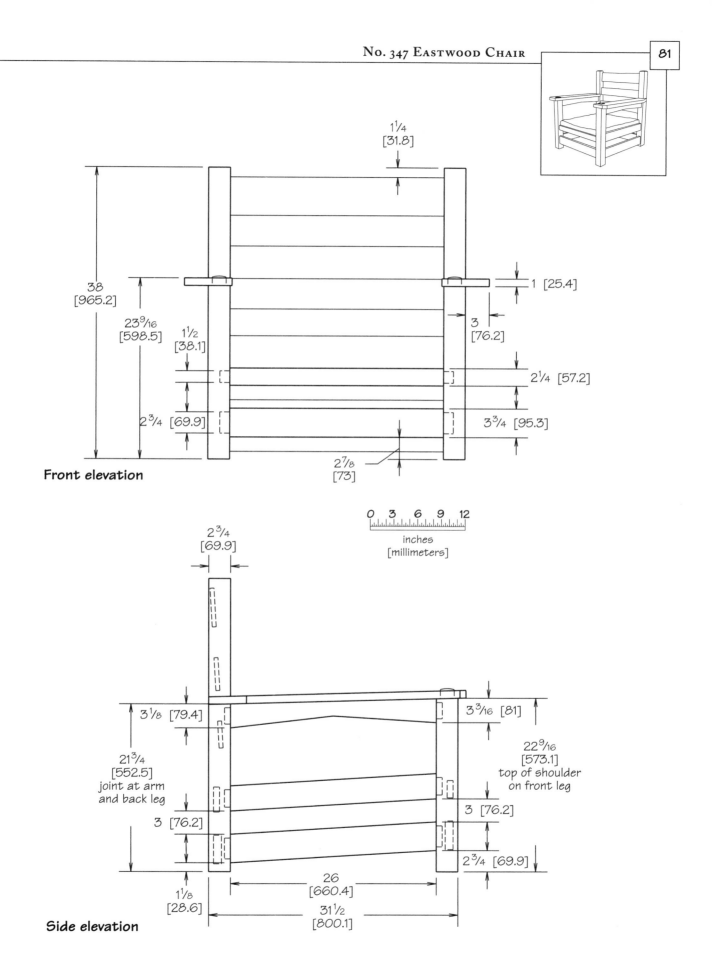

Front elevation

38 [965.2]

23⁹/₁₆ [598.5]

1¹/₂ [38.1]

2³/₄ [69.9]

1¹/₄ [31.8]

1 [25.4]

3 [76.2]

2¹/₄ [57.2]

3³/₄ [95.3]

2⁷/₈ [73]

0 3 6 9 12
inches
[millimeters]

Side elevation

2³/₄ [69.9]

3¹/₈ [79.4]

21³/₄ [552.5]
joint at arm
and back leg

3 [76.2]

1¹/₈ [28.6]

3³/₁₆ [81]

22⁹/₁₆ [573.1]
top of shoulder
on front leg

3 [76.2]

2³/₄ [69.9]

26 [660.4]

31¹/₂ [800.1]

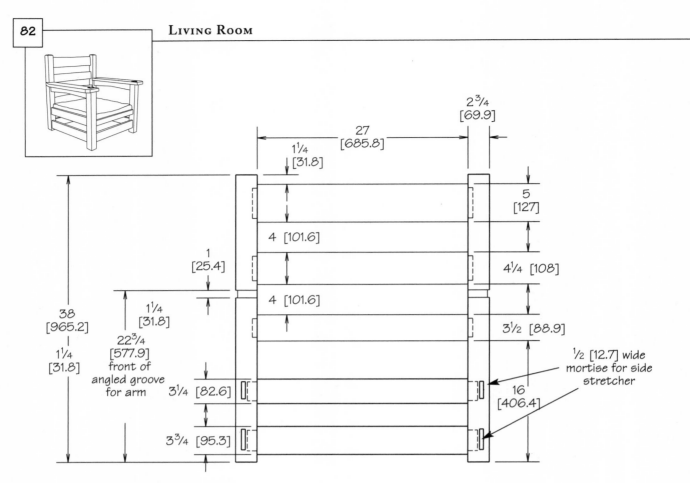

Elevation of assembled back- viewed from the front

27 [685.8]

2³/4 [69.9]

1¼ [31.8]

5 [127]

4 [101.6]

4¼ [108]

1 [25.4]

4 [101.6]

3½ [88.9]

1¼ [31.8]

38 [965.2]

22³/4 [577.9] front of angled groove for arm

½ [12.7] wide mortise for side stretcher

1¼ [31.8]

3¼ [82.6]

16 [406.4]

3³/4 [95.3]

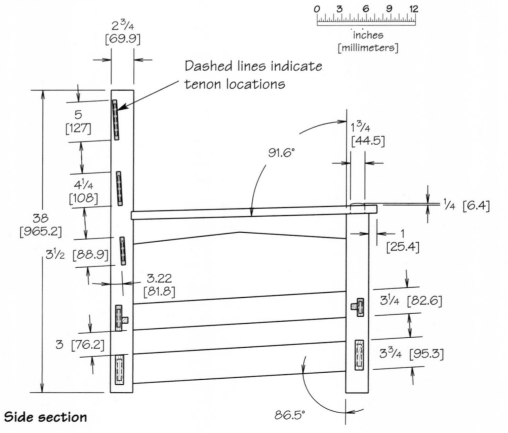

Side section

2³/4 [69.9]

Dashed lines indicate tenon locations

5 [127]

1³/4 [44.5]

91.6°

4¼ [108]

¼ [6.4]

38 [965.2]

1 [25.4]

3½ [88.9]

3.22 [81.8]

3¼ [82.6]

3 [76.2]

3³/4 [95.3]

86.5°

0 3 6 9 12
inches
[millimeters]

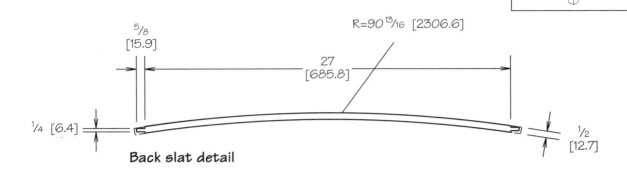

5/8
[15.9]

R=90 13/16 [2306.6]

27
[685.8]

1/4 [6.4]

1/2
[12.7]

Back slat detail

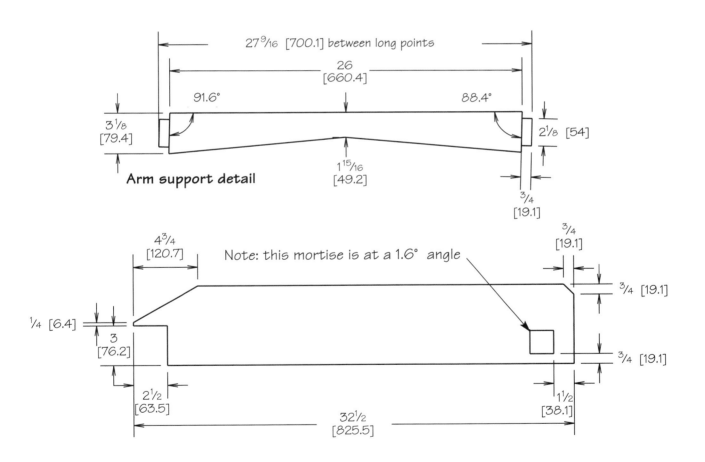

27 9/16 [700.1] between long points

26
[660.4]

91.6°   88.4°

3 1/8
[79.4]

2 1/8 [54]

Arm support detail

1 15/16
[49.2]

3/4
[19.1]

4 3/4
[120.7]

Note: this mortise is at a 1.6° angle

3/4
[19.1]

3/4 [19.1]

1/4 [6.4]

3
[76.2]

3/4 [19.1]

2 1/2
[63.5]

1 1/2
[38.1]

32 1/2
[825.5]

"True" plan of arm

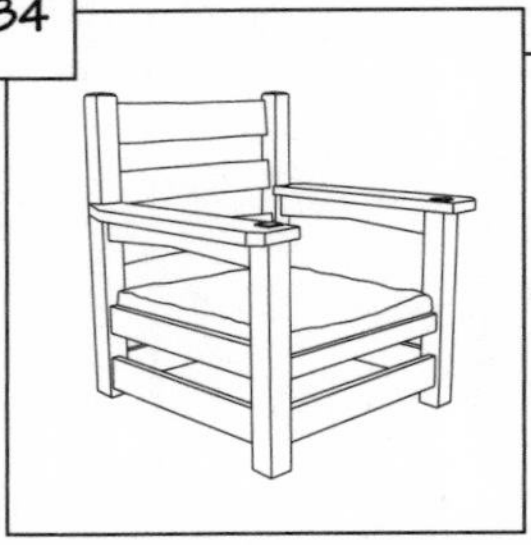

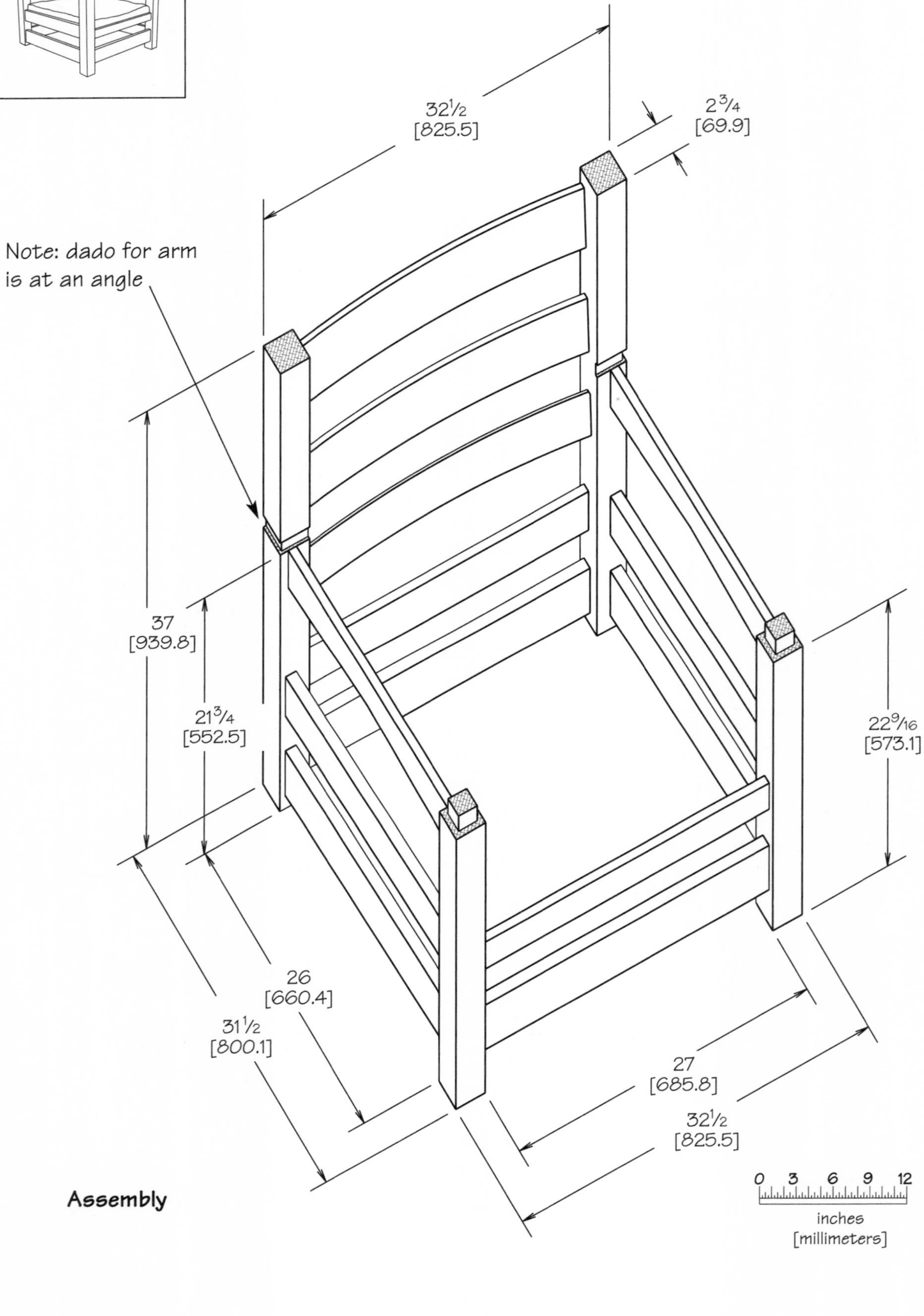

Note: dado for arm
is at an angle

32½
[825.5]

2¾
[69.9]

37
[939.8]

21¾
[552.5]

22⁹⁄₁₆
[573.1]

26
[660.4]

31½
[800.1]

27
[685.8]

32½
[825.5]

Assembly

0 3 6 9 12

inches
[millimeters]

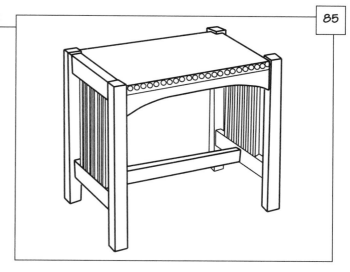

L. & J. G. STICKLEY
NO. 1292 FOOTSTOOL

18 x 13 x 16 high [457 x 330 x 406]

Note that the leather top is tucked in at the ends, and overlays the arched top rail at the front and back, held down with decorative tacks. Make it as a slip seat, but leave the long edges of the leather loose. After the stool is finished, attach the seat, fold the leather over the edges, trim it straight, and tack it down.

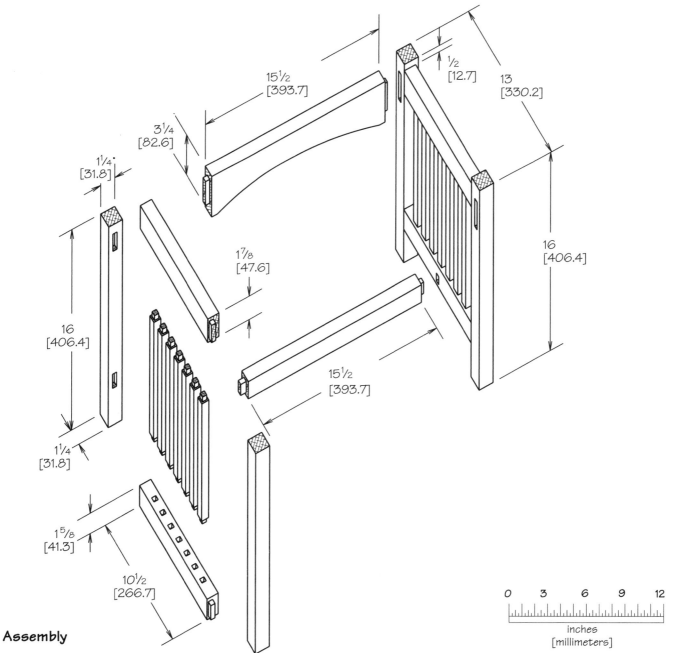

15½ [393.7]

3¼ [82.6]

1¼ [31.8]

½ [12.7]

13 [330.2]

1⅞ [47.6]

16 [406.4]

16 [406.4]

16 [406.4]

1¼ [31.8]

15½ [393.7]

1⅝ [41.3]

10½ [266.7]

0 3 6 9 12

inches
[millimeters]

Assembly

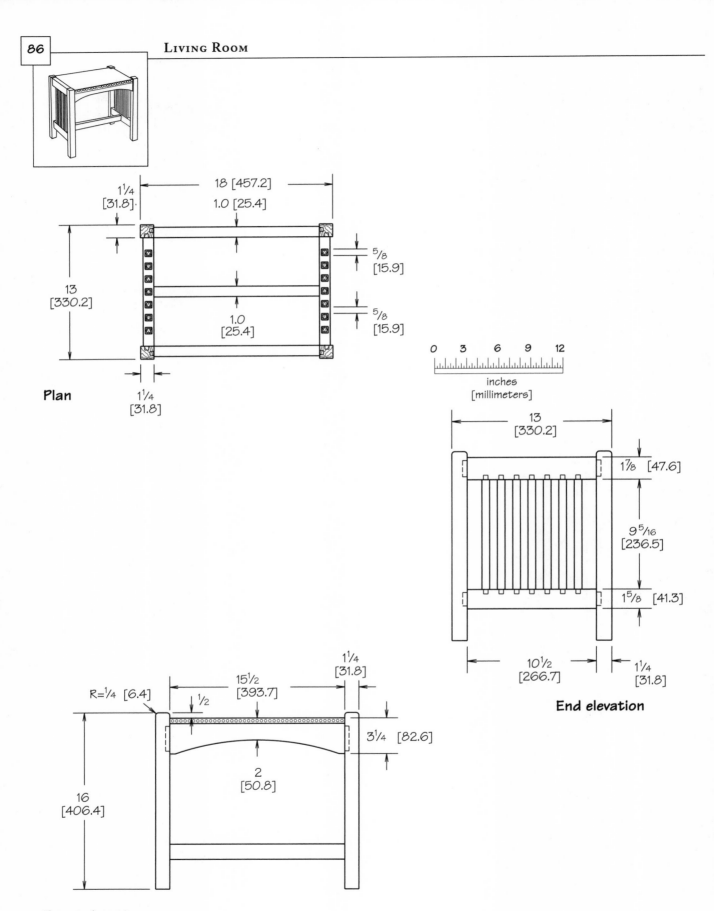

Plan

1 1/4 [31.8]

18 [457.2]

1.0 [25.4]

5/8 [15.9]

5/8 [15.9]

1.0 [25.4]

13 [330.2]

1 1/4 [31.8]

0 3 6 9 12

inches
[millimeters]

13 [330.2]

1 7/8 [47.6]

9 5/16 [236.5]

1 5/8 [41.3]

10 1/2 [266.7]

1 1/4 [31.8]

End elevation

R=1/4 [6.4]

15 1/2 [393.7]

1 1/4 [31.8]

1/2

3 1/4 [82.6]

2 [50.8]

16 [406.4]

Front elevation

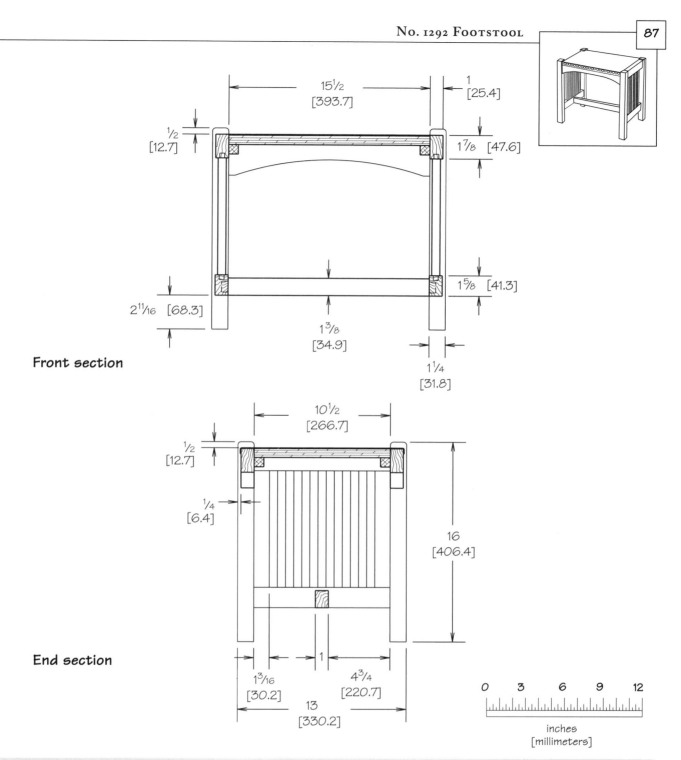

Front section

15½ [393.7]
1 [25.4]
½ [12.7]
1⁷⁄₈ [47.6]
2¹¹⁄₁₆ [68.3]
1⁵⁄₈ [41.3]
1³⁄₈ [34.9]
1¼ [31.8]

End section

10½ [266.7]
½ [12.7]
¼ [6.4]
16 [406.4]
1
1³⁄₁₆ [30.2]
4³⁄₄ [220.7]
13 [330.2]

0 3 6 9 12

inches
[millimeters]

L & J. G. Stickley No. 1292 Footstool

Qty	Part	Size		Notes
4	legs	1¼ x 1¼ x 16	[31.8 x 31.8 x 406.4]	
2	bottom rails	1 x 1⁵⁄₈ x 11½	[25.4 x 41.3 x 292.1]	10½ [266.7] between tenons
2	top rails	1 x 1⁷⁄₈ x 11½	[25.4 x 47.6 x 292.1]	10½ [266.7] between tenons
14	spindles	⁵⁄₈ x ⁵⁄₈ x 10¹⁄₁₆	[15.9 x 15.9 x 255.6]	9⁵⁄₁₆ [236.5] between tenons
2	arched rails	1 x 3¼ x 16½	[25.4 x 82.6 x 419.1]	15½ [393.7] between tenons
1	stretcher	1 x 1³⁄₈ x 16½	[25.4 x 34.9 x 419.1]	15½ [393.7] between tenons
1	top	¾ x 10½ x 15½	[19.1 x 266.7 x 393.7]	plywood or assembled frame for upholstery

GUSTAV STICKLEY NO. 206 SETTLE
60 wide x 40 high x 28 deep [1524 x 1016 x 711]

This love-seat size settle is unusual because of the rounded tops of the rails, and the angle of the back and sides. These features make it more comfortable than similar settles. The original seat cushion was supported by woven cane, and was available upholstered in "Craftsman Canvas" or leather.

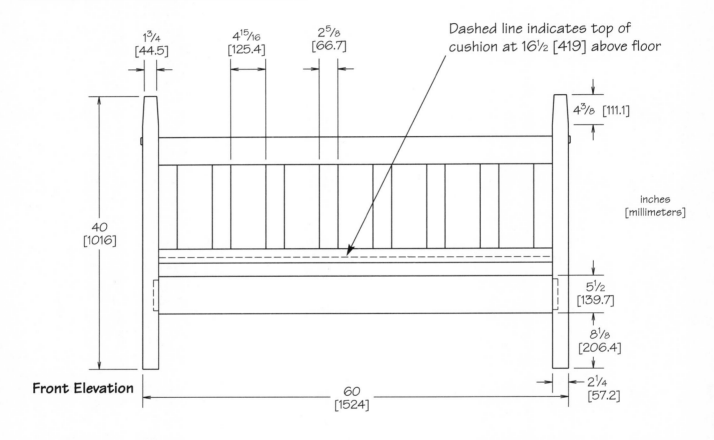

Dashed line indicates top of cushion at 16½ [419] above floor

Front Elevation

inches [millimeters]

Gustav Stickley No. 206 Settle

QTY	PART	SIZE		NOTES
4	legs	2¼ x 2¼ x 40	[57.2 x 57.2 x 1016]	
2	lower front & back rails	1¼ x 5½ x 57	[31.8 x 139.7 x 1448]	55½ [1410] between tenons
2	lower side rails	1¼ x 5½ x 25	[31.8 x 139.7 x 635]	23½ [597] between tenons
2	middle side rails	1 x 2⅛ x 24½	[25.4 x 54 x 622.3]	23½ [597] between tenons
2	top side rails	1 x 2½ x 24½	[25.4 x 63.5 x 622.3]	23½ [597] between tenons
2	side rail caps	1⅛ x 2⅛ x 23½	[28.6 x 54 x 597]	
1	middle back rail	1 x 2⅛ x 56½	[25.4 x 54 x 1435]	55½ [1410] between tenons
1	top back rail	1 x 2½ x 56½	[25.4 x 63.5 x 1435]	55½ [1410] between tenons
1	back rail cap	1⅛ x 2⅛ x 55½	[28.6 x 54 x 1410]	
6	side slats	⅝ x 4¹⁵⁄₁₆ x 13¼	[15.9 x 125.4 x 336.5]	12¼ [311.2] between tenons
7	back slats	⅝ x 4¹⁵⁄₁₆ x 13¼	[15.9 x 125.4 x 336.5]	12¼ [311.2] between tenons

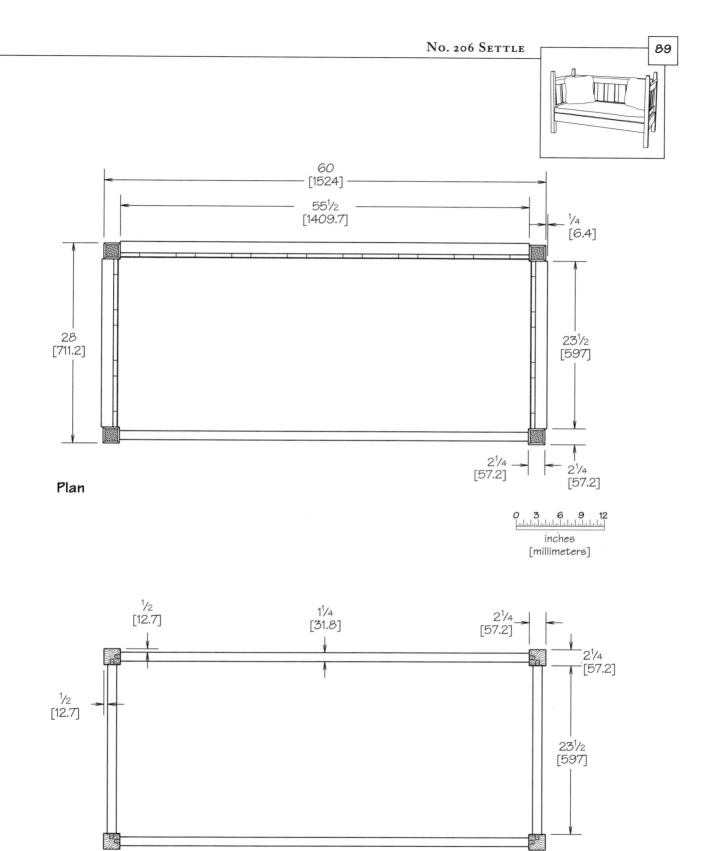

60
[1524]

55½
[1409.7]

¼
[6.4]

28
[711.2]

23½
[597]

2¼
[57.2]

2¼
[57.2]

Plan

0   3   6   9   12
inches
[millimeters]

½
[12.7]

1¼
[31.8]

2¼
[57.2]

2¼
[57.2]

½
[12.7]

23½
[597]

55½
[1409.7]

Plan section at seat

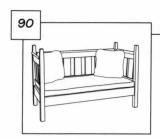

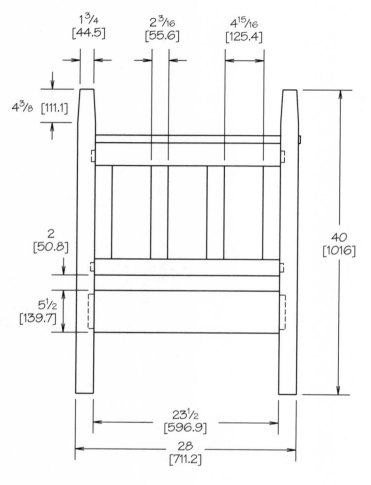

1³/₄ [44.5]

2³/₁₆ [55.6]

4¹⁵/₁₆ [125.4]

4³/₈ [111.1]

2 [50.8]

5¹/₂ [139.7]

40 [1016]

23¹/₂ [596.9]

28 [711.2]

Side elevation

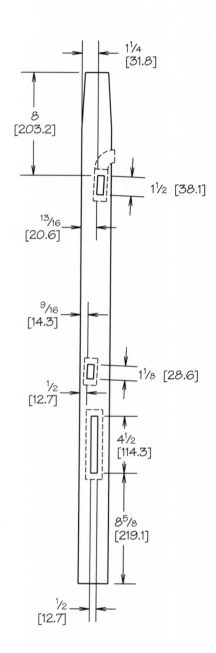

1¹/₄ [31.8]

8 [203.2]

1¹/₂ [38.1]

13/₁₆ [20.6]

9/₁₆ [14.3]

1¹/₈ [28.6]

¹/₂ [12.7]

4¹/₂ [114.3]

8⁵/₈ [219.1]

¹/₂ [12.7]

Detail-mortise locations on leg

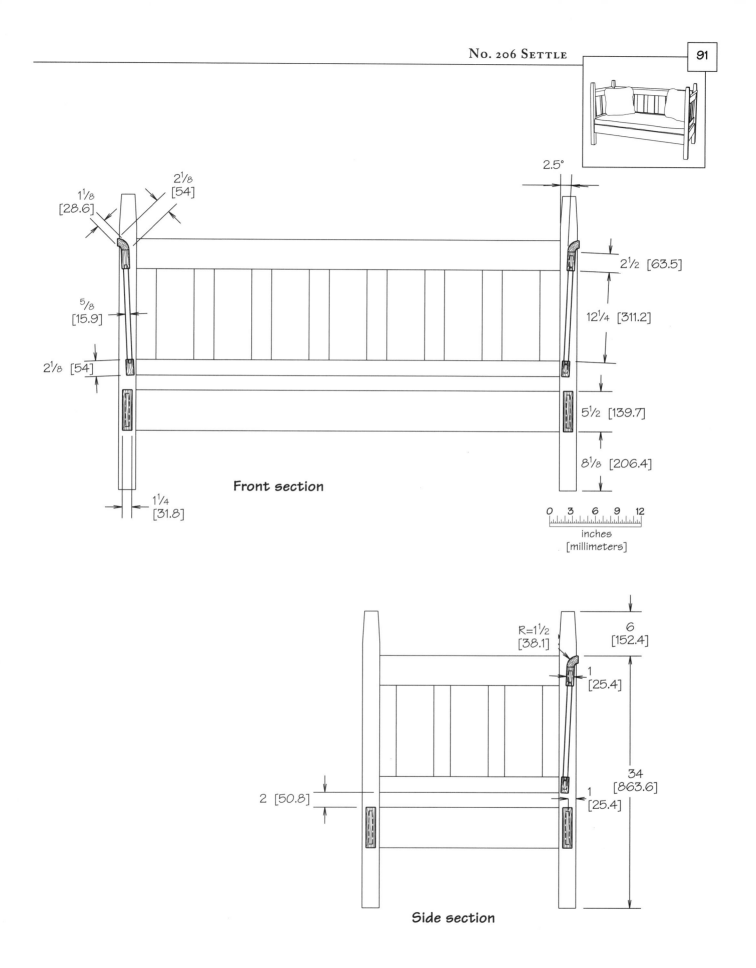

2.5°

1⅛
[28.6]

2⅛
[54]

2½ [63.5]

5/8
[15.9]

12¼ [311.2]

2⅛ [54]

5½ [139.7]

8⅛ [206.4]

Front section

1¼
[31.8]

0 3 6 9 12

inches
[millimeters]

R=1½
[38.1]

6
[152.4]

1
[25.4]

34
[863.6]

2 [50.8]

1
[25.4]

Side section

L. & J. G. STICKLEY NO. 225 SETTLE

47 1/8 wide x 22 3/4 deep x 36 1/2 high
[1197 wide x 578 deep x 927 high]

The original catalog description speaks of this having a "spring seat cushion." There is enough space below the top rails for a frame with sinuous wire springs attached, or a simple cushion supported by slats could be used.

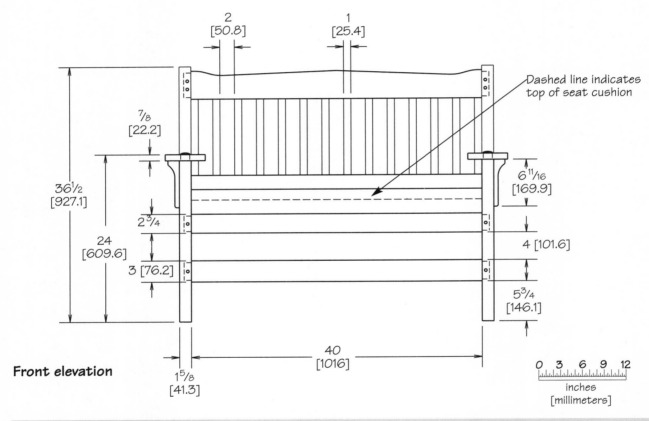

Dashed line indicates top of seat cushion

Front elevation

L. & J. G. Stickley No. 225 Settle

QTY	PART	SIZE		NOTES
2	front legs	1 5/8 x 1 5/8 x 24 1/4	[41.3 x 41.3 x 616	23 1/8 [587.4] below shoulder under arm
2	back legs	1 5/8 x 3 3/16 x 36 1/2	[41.3 x 81 x 927.1]	
2	lwr front & back rail	1 x 3 x 42	[25.4 x 76.2 x 1066.8]	40 [1041.4] between tenons
2	front & back seat rail	1 x 2 3/4 x 42	[25.4 x 69.9 x 1066.8]	40 [1041.4] between tenons
2	lower side rails	1 x 2 x 19 1/4	[25.4 x 50.8 x 489]	17 1/4 [438.2] between tenons
2	side seat rails	1 x 2 3/4 x 19 1/4	[25.4 x 69.9 x 489]	17 1/4 [438.2] between tenons
2	arms	7/8 x 5 1/2 x 21 1/4	[22.2 x 139.7 x 539.8]	
1	lower back rail	1 x 2 x 42	[25.4 x 50.8 x 1066.8]	40 [1041.4] between tenons
1	upper back rail	1 x 4 x 42	[25.4 x 101.6 x 1066.8]	40 [1041.4] between tenons
13	back slats	1/2 x 2 x 11 15/16	[12.7 x 50.8 x 303.2]	10 15/16 [277.8] between tenons
2	corbels	7/8 x 1 5/8 x 6 11/16	[22.2 x 41.3 x 169.9]	

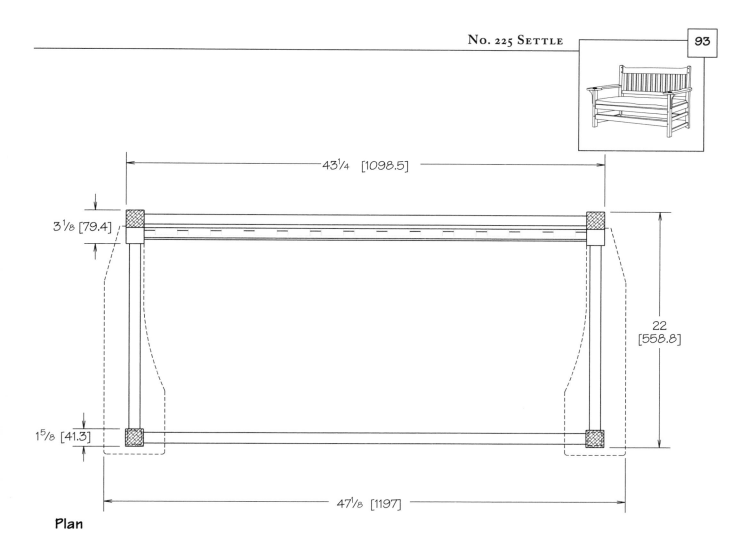

43¼ [1098.5]

3⅛ [79.4]

22 [558.8]

1⅝ [41.3]

47⅛ [1197]

Plan

Plan of Arm
Grid = 1" [25.4mm] squares

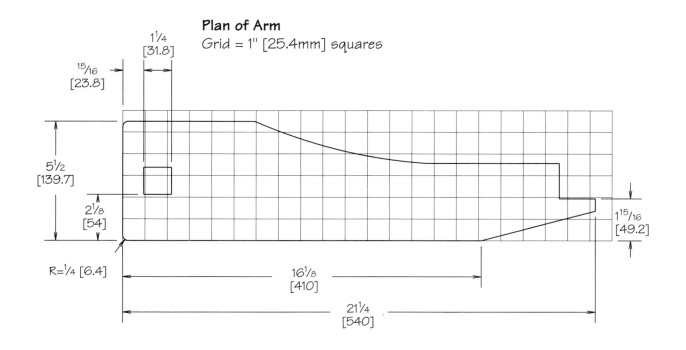

1¼ [31.8]

15/16 [23.8]

5½ [139.7]

2⅛ [54]

R=¼ [6.4]

16⅛ [410]

21¼ [540]

1¹⁵/₁₆ [49.2]

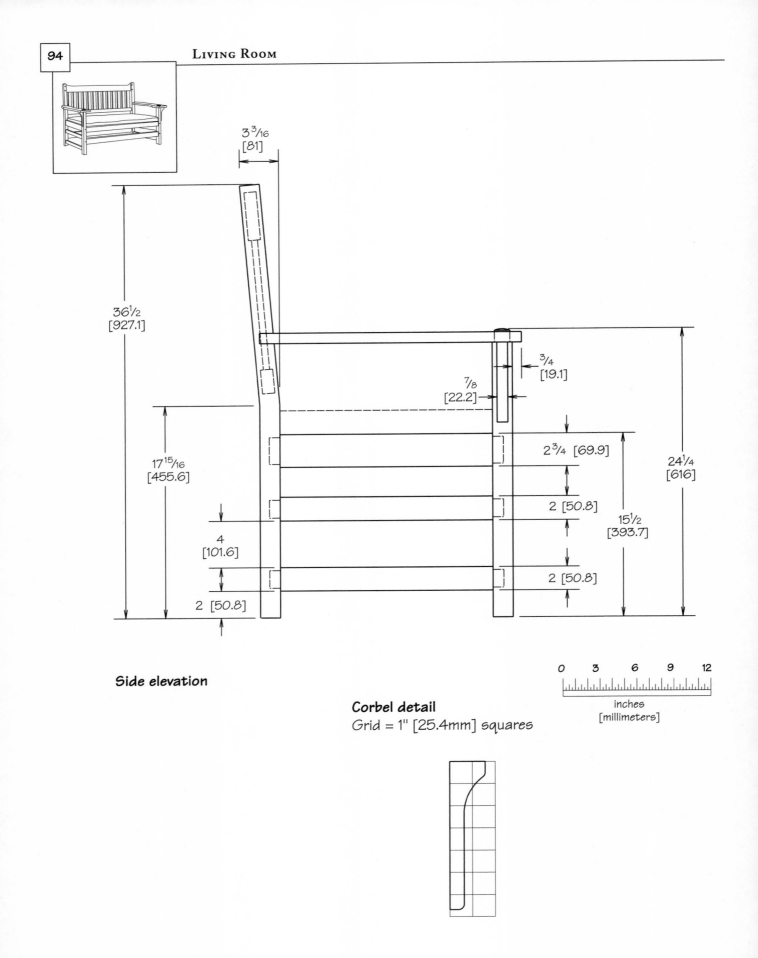

3 3/16
[81]

36 1/2
[927.1]

17 15/16
[455.6]

4
[101.6]

2 [50.8]

3/4
[19.1]

7/8
[22.2]

2 3/4 [69.9]

2 [50.8]

2 [50.8]

24 1/4
[616]

15 1/2
[393.7]

Side elevation

0 3 6 9 12

inches
[millimeters]

Corbel detail
Grid = 1" [25.4mm] squares

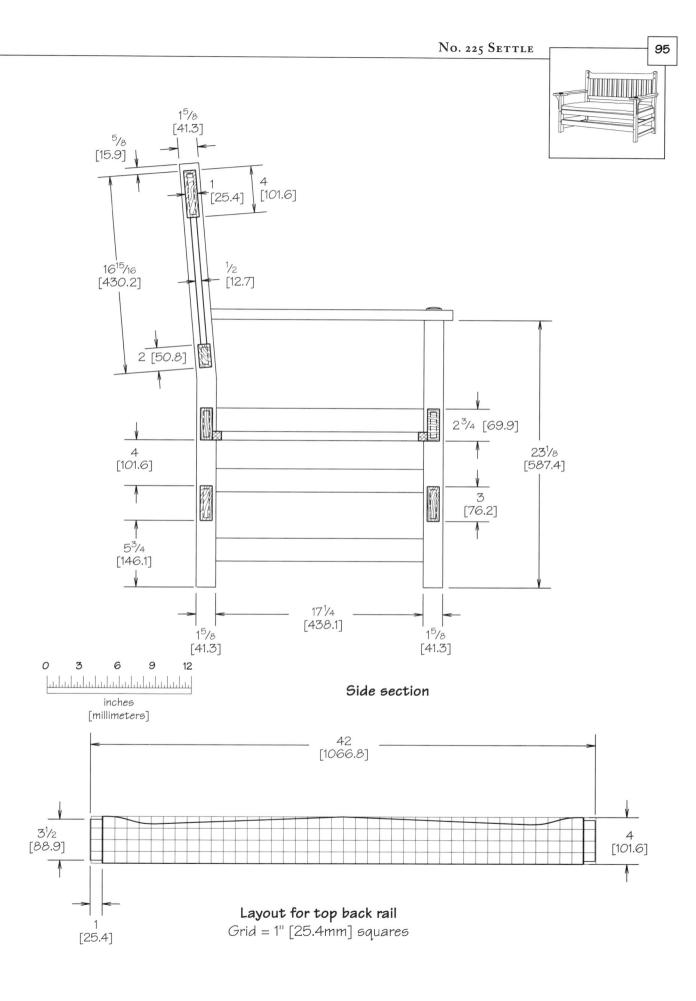

1⁵⁄₈ [41.3]

⁵⁄₈ [15.9]

1 [25.4]

4 [101.6]

16¹⁵⁄₁₆ [430.2]

½ [12.7]

2 [50.8]

2³⁄₄ [69.9]

23⅛ [587.4]

4 [101.6]

3 [76.2]

5³⁄₄ [146.1]

17¼ [438.1]

1⁵⁄₈ [41.3]

1⁵⁄₈ [41.3]

0 3 6 9 12

inches [millimeters]

Side section

42 [1066.8]

3½ [88.9]

4 [101.6]

1 [25.4]

Layout for top back rail
Grid = 1" [25.4mm] squares

BEDROOM

No. 911 Dresser with Mirror   98

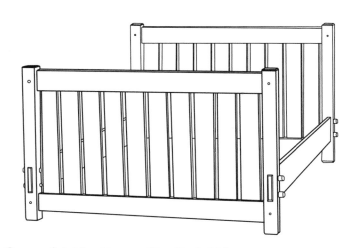

Gustav Stickley Queen-Size Bed   103

Limbert Vanity Table with Mirror   108

No. 110 Nightstand   113

GUSTAV STICKLEY
NO. 911 DRESSER

33 high (to top of case) x 48 wide x 20 deep
{838 x 1219 x 508]

Another elegant Harvey Ellis design. The butterfly keys holding the support for the mirror together stand slightly proud, and the mirror frame is attached with cleats screwed to the back of the case. The mirror pivots on fittings that were common on all types of furniture of the period. Like the 913 dresser, the side panels can be stiles and rails, or a simple veneered panel.

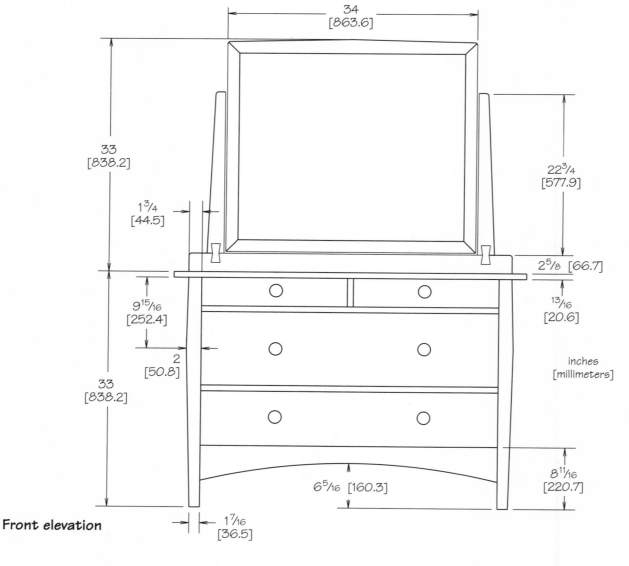

inches
[millimeters]

Front elevation

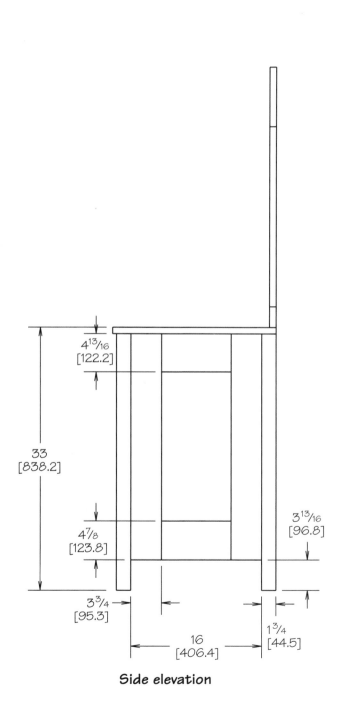

4¹³⁄₁₆
[122.2]

33
[838.2]

4⁷⁄₈
[123.8]

3¹³⁄₁₆
[96.8]

3¾
[95.3]

16
[406.4]

1¾
[44.5]

Side elevation

2
[50.8]

30⅛
[765.2]

½
[12.7]

2⅛
[54]

66
[1676.4]

4
[101.6]

10¼
[260.4]

7⅝
[193.7]

19½
[495.3]

Side section

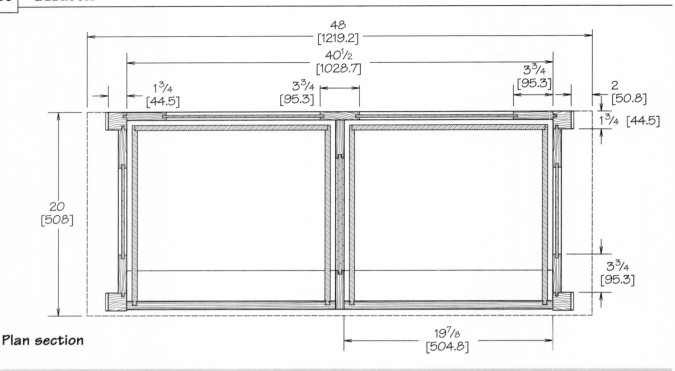

Plan section

Gustav Stickley No. 911 Dresser

QTY	PART	SIZE		NOTES
1	top	$^{13}/_{16}$ x 20 x 48	[20.6 x 508 x 1219.2]	
4	legs	$1^3/_4$ x 2 x $32^3/_{16}$	[44.5 x 50.8 x 817.6]	
2	side panels	$^3/_4$ x $16^3/_4$ x $28^3/_8$	[19.1 x 425.5 x 720.7]	assembled-16 x $28^3/_8$ [406.4 x 720.7] exposed-parts detailed below
4	stiles	$^3/_4$ x $4^1/_8$ x $28^3/_8$	[19.1 x 104.8 x 720.7]	$3^3/_4$ [95.3] exposed
2	bottom rails	$^3/_4$ x $4^7/_8$ x $9^1/_2$	[19.1 x 123.8 x 241.3]	$8^1/_2$ [215.9] between tenons
2	top rails	$^3/_4$ x $4^{13}/_{16}$ x $9^1/_2$	[19.1 x 122.2 x 241.3]	$8^1/_2$ [215.9] between tenons
2	panels	$^1/_4$ x $9^1/_2$ x $19^{11}/_{16}$	[6.4 x 241.3 x 500.1]	$8^1/_2$ x $18^{11}/_{16}$ [215.9 x 474.7] exposed
1	back panel	$^3/_4$ x $41^1/_2$ x $28^3/_8$	[19.1 x 1054.1 x 720.7]	assembled-$40^1/_2$ [1028.7] exposed-parts detailed below
2	stiles	$^3/_4$ x $4^1/_8$ x $28^3/_8$	[19.1 x 104.8 x 720.7]	$3^3/_4$ [95.3] exposed
2	rails	$^3/_4$ x $3^3/_4$ x $33^3/_4$	[19.1 x 95.3 x 857.3]	33 [838.2] between tenons
1	mid stile	$^3/_4$ x $3^3/_4$ x $21^5/_8$	[19.1 x 95.3 x 549.3]	$20^7/_8$ [530.2] between tenons
2	panels	$^1/_4$ x $15^3/_8$ x $21^5/_8$	[6.4 x 390.5 x 549.3]	$14^5/_8$ x $20^7/_8$ [371.5 x 530.2] exposed
1	arched apron	$^3/_4$ x $4^7/_8$ x $42^1/_2$	[19.1 x 123.8 x 1079.5]	$40^1/_2$ [1028.7] between tenons
1	bottom drawer front	$^3/_4$ x $7^5/_8$ x $40^1/_2$	[19.1 x 193.7 x 1028.7]	opening
1	middle drawer front	$^3/_4$ x $10^1/_4$ x $40^1/_2$	[19.1 x 260.4 x 1028.7]	opening
2	top drawer fronts	$^3/_4$ x 4 x $19^7/_8$	[19.1 x 101.6 x 504.8]	opening
1	bottom rail	$^3/_4$ x $2^1/_4$ x $42^1/_2$	[19.1 x 57.2 x 1079.5]	$40^1/_2$ [1028.7] between tenons
2	middle rails	$^3/_4$ x $3^1/_4$ x $42^1/_2$	[19.1 x 82.6 x 1079.5]	$40^1/_2$ [1028.7] between tenons
2	top rails	$^3/_4$ x $3^1/_4$ x $19^7/_8$	[19.1 x 82.6 x 504.8]	add for tenons or pocket screw
1	vertical divider	$^3/_4$ x $18^5/_8$ x 4	[19.1 x 473.1 x 101.6]	vertical grain on front exposed edge
1	backsplash	$^3/_4$ x $2^5/_8$ x 44	[19.1 x 66.7 x 1117.6]	
2	mirror supports	$^3/_4$ x $2^5/_{16}$ x $22^3/_4$	[19.1 x 58.7 x 577.9]	
2	mirror stiles	$^3/_4$ x $1^5/_8$ x $29^3/_4$	[19.1 x 41.3 x 755.7]	
1	mirror bottom rail	$^3/_4$ x $1^5/_8$ x 34	[19.1 x 41.3 x 863.6]	
1	mirror top rail	$^3/_4$ x 2 x 34	[19.1 x 50.8 x 863.6]	taper to $1^5/_8$ [41.3] at ends

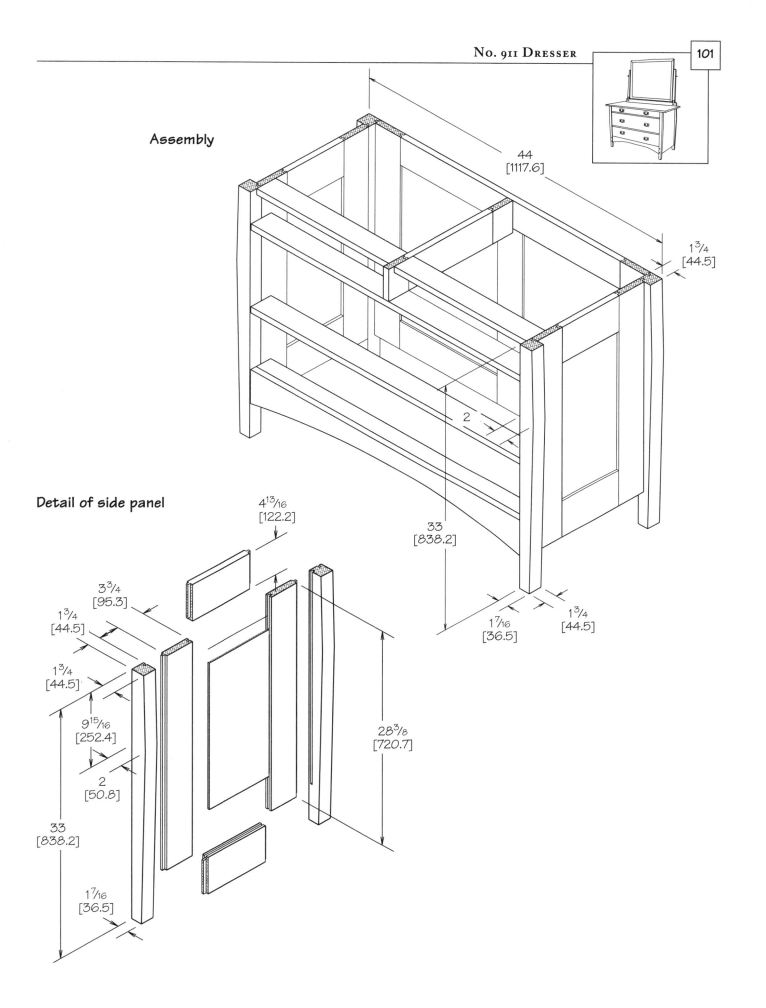

Assembly

44
[1117.6]

1³/₄
[44.5]

2

33
[838.2]

1⁷/₁₆
[36.5]

1³/₄
[44.5]

Detail of side panel

4¹³/₁₆
[122.2]

3³/₄
[95.3]

1³/₄
[44.5]

1³/₄
[44.5]

9¹⁵/₁₆
[252.4]

2
[50.8]

33
[838.2]

1⁷/₁₆
[36.5]

28³/₈
[720.7]

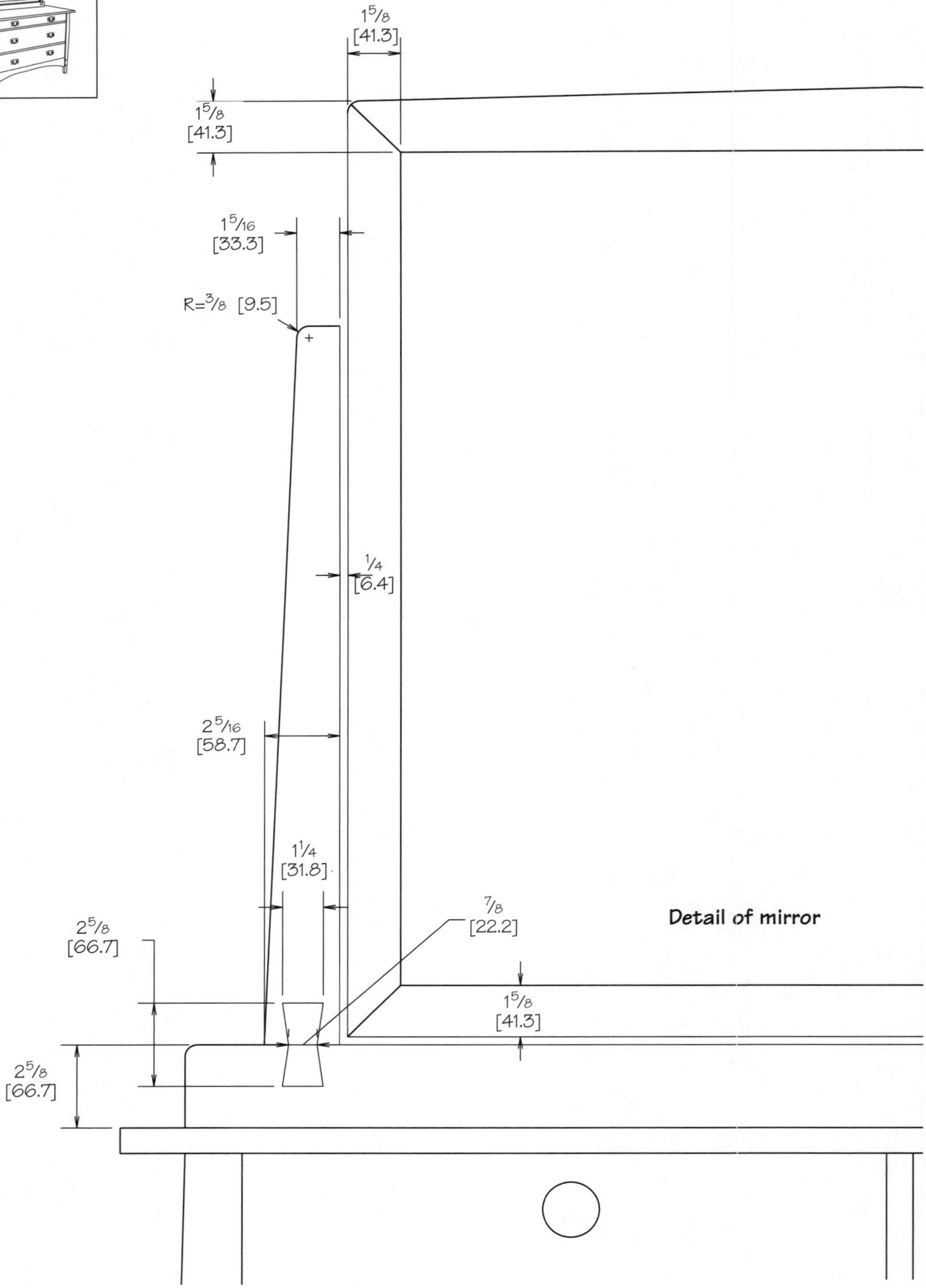

$1\frac{5}{8}$
[41.3]

$1\frac{5}{8}$
[41.3]

$1\frac{5}{16}$
[33.3]

$R=\frac{3}{8}$ [9.5]

$\frac{1}{4}$
[6.4]

$2\frac{5}{16}$
[58.7]

$1\frac{1}{4}$
[31.8]

$\frac{7}{8}$
[22.2]

Detail of mirror

$2\frac{5}{8}$
[66.7]

$1\frac{5}{8}$
[41.3]

$2\frac{5}{8}$
[66.7]

BED BY GUSTAV STICKLEY

87.5 long x 65 wide x 42.5 high
[2222 x 1650 x 1080]

A different approach to fastening the rails to
the head and footboard — the removable pegs
lock the through tenons of the rails to the
head and footboard. These joints should not
be glued. The head and foot board are identical. Dimensions have been modified slightly
to accommodate a modern queen size mattress
— before you begin construction, check the fit
of the particular mattress you will be using.

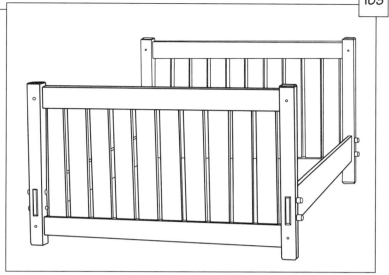

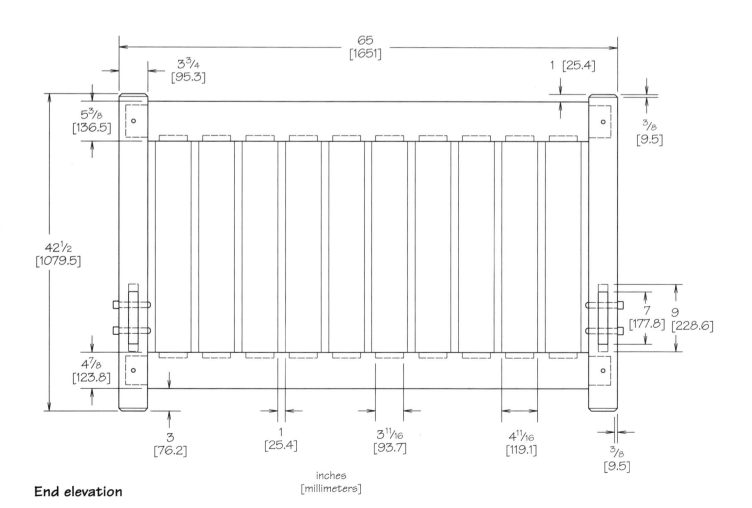

End elevation

inches
[millimeters]

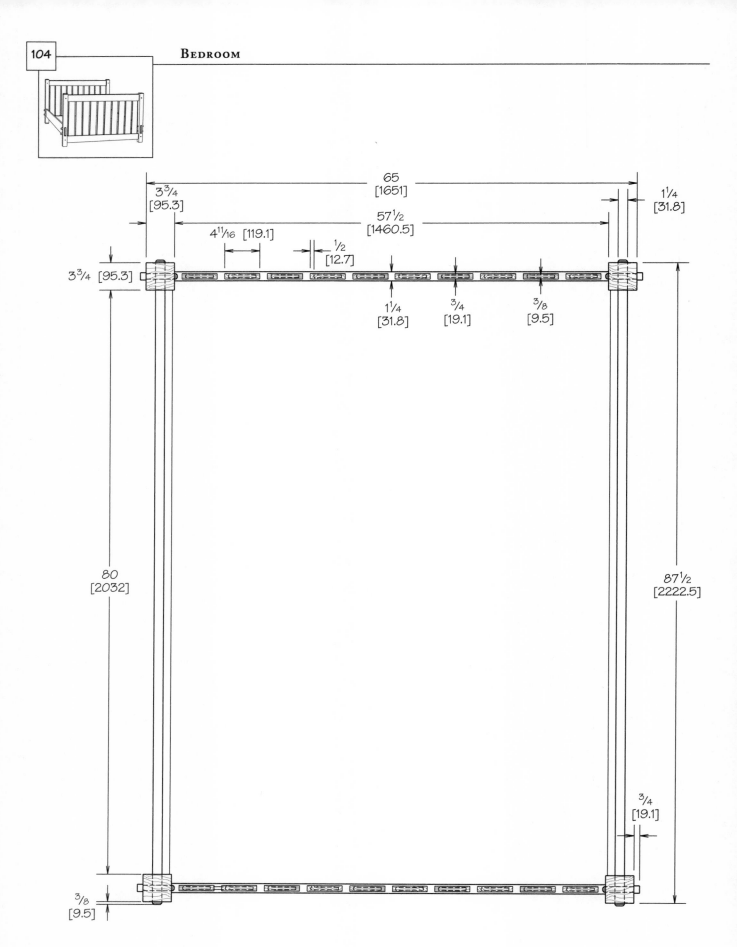

65
[1651]

3³/₄
[95.3]

1¹/₄
[31.8]

57¹/₂
[1460.5]

4¹¹/₁₆ [119.1]

¹/₂
[12.7]

3³/₄ [95.3]

1¹/₄
[31.8]

³/₄
[19.1]

³/₈
[9.5]

80
[2032]

87¹/₂
[2222.5]

³/₄
[19.1]

³/₈
[9.5]

Plan

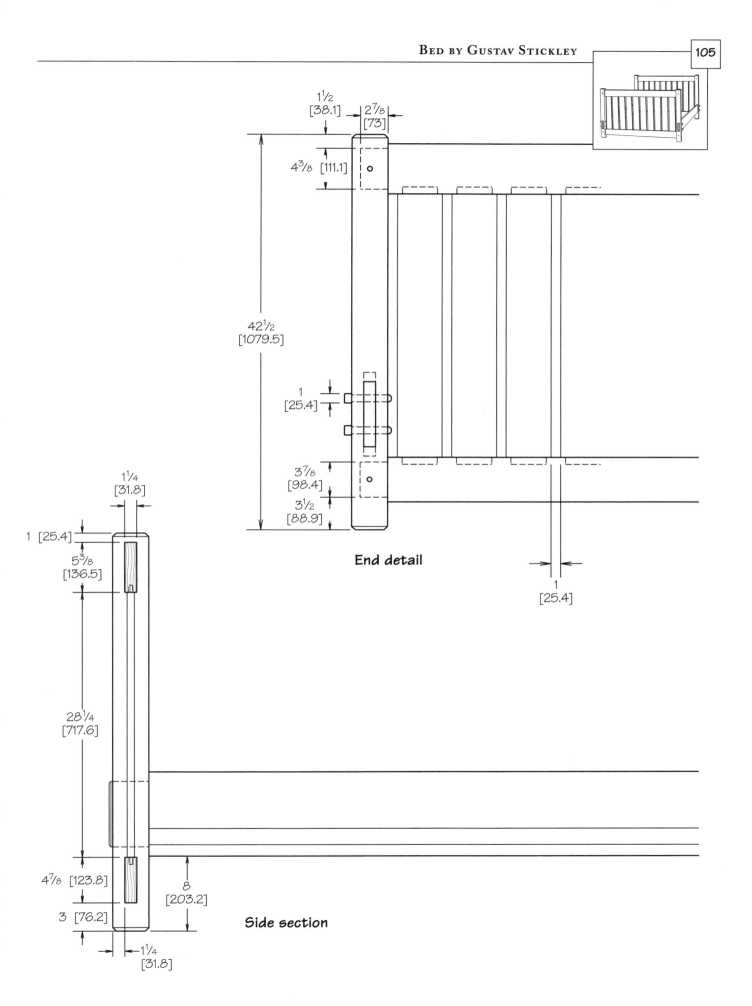

1½
[38.1]

2⅞
[73]

4³⁄₈ [111.1]

42½
[1079.5]

1
[25.4]

3⅞
[98.4]

3½
[88.9]

End detail

1
[25.4]

1¼
[31.8]

1 [25.4]

5³⁄₈
[136.5]

28¼
[717.6]

4⅞ [123.8]

8
[203.2]

3 [76.2]

Side section

1¼
[31.8]

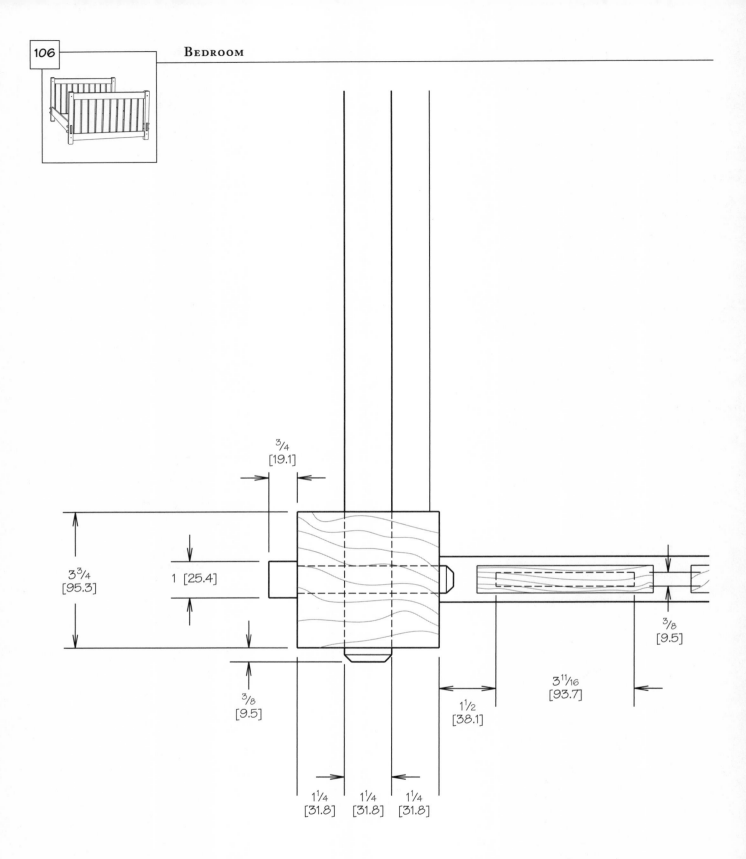

3/4 [19.1]

3³/₄ [95.3]

1 [25.4]

3/8 [9.5]

3/8 [9.5]

3¹¹/₁₆ [93.7]

1¹/₂ [38.1]

1¹/₄ [31.8]   1¹/₄ [31.8]   1¹/₄ [31.8]

Joint details - plan view

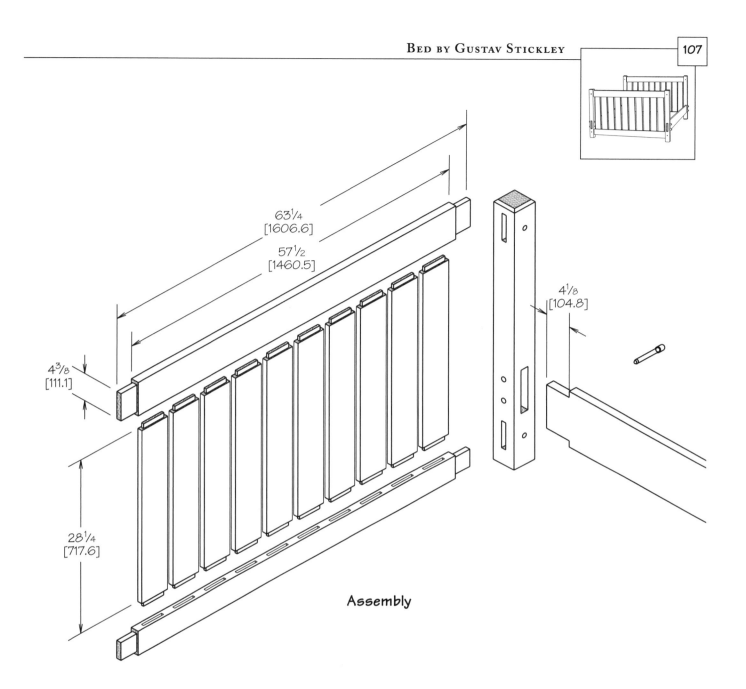

63¹/₄
[1606.6]

57¹/₂
[1460.5]

4³/₈
[111.1]

28¹/₄
[717.6]

4¹/₈
[104.8]

Assembly

Bed by Gustav Stickley

Qty	Part	Size		Notes
4	posts	3³/₄ x 3³/₄ x 42¹/₂	[95.3 x 95.3 x 1079.5]	
2	bottom rails	1¹/₄ x 4⁷/₈ x 63¹/₂	[31.8 x 123.8 x 1613.0]	57¹/₂ [1460] between tenons
2	top rails	1¹/₄ x 5³/₈ x 63¹/₂	[31.8 x 136.5 x 1613.0]	57¹/₂ [1460] between tenons
20	vertical slats	³/₄ x 4¹¹/₁₆ x 29³/₄	[19.1 x 119.0 x 755.6]	28¹/₄ [717.5] between tenons
2	rails	1¹/₄ x 9 x 87¹/₂	[31.8 x 228.6 x 2222.5]	80 [2032] between tenons — check length against mattress

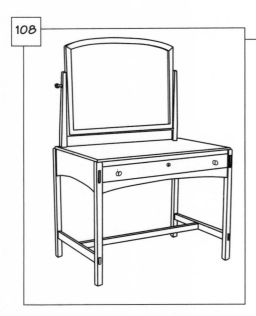

CHARLES LIMBERT DRESSING TABLE
30 high x 36 wide x 24 deep [762 x 914 x 610]

All of the exposed edges are rounded over, a look that became newly popular in the 1970s. The exposed tenons are also rounded, with a smaller radius. The top is stepped in, and sits in a $^{1}/_{8}$" [3.2] deep rabbet around the top edge of the frame.

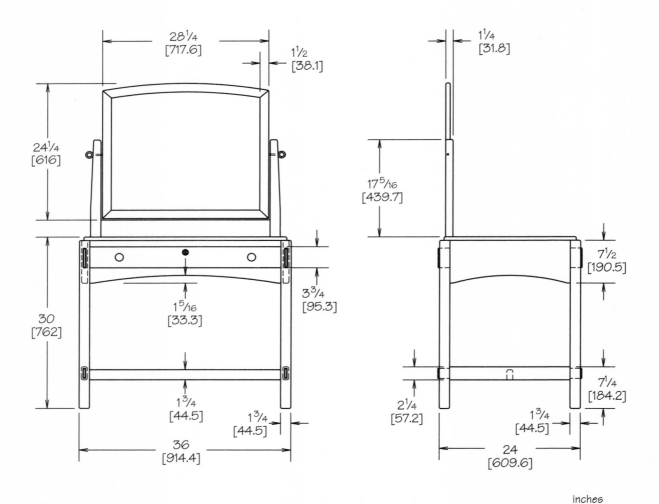

Front Elevation

Side elevation

inches
[millimeters]

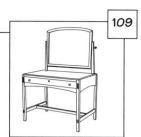
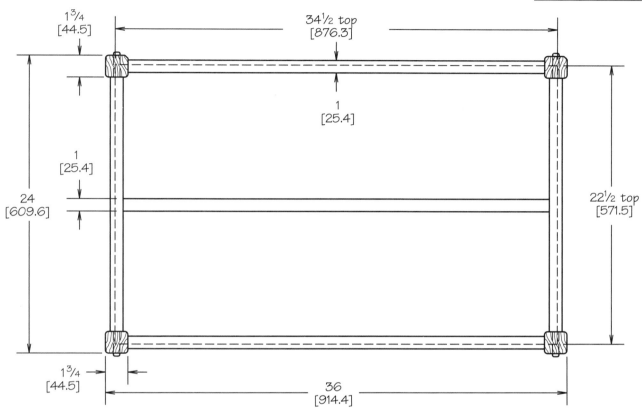

Plan section above stretcher

Charles Limbert Dressing Table

QTY	PART	SIZE		NOTES
4	legs	$1^3/4$ x $1^3/4$ x $29^3/8$	[44.5 x 44.5 x 746.1]	
2	side stretchers	1 x $2^1/4$ x $24^1/2$	[25.4 x 57.2 x 622.3]	$20^1/2$ [520.7] between tenons
1	stretcher	1 x $1^3/4$ x 34 $1/4$	[25.4 x 44.5 x 870]	$33^1/4$ [844.6] between tenons
2	arched side rails	1 x $7^1/2$ x $24^1/2$	[25.4 x 190.5 x 622.3]	$20^1/2$ [520.7] between tenons
1	back rail	1 x $7^1/2$ x $34^1/4$	[25.4 x 190.5 x 870]	$33^1/4$ [844.6] between tenons
1	arched front rail	1 x $2^5/8$ x $34^1/4$	[25.4 x 66.7 x 870]	$33^1/4$ [844.6] between tenons
1	top	$3/4$ x $22^1/2$ x $34^1/2$	[19.1 x 571.5 x 876.3]	
1	drawer front	1 x $3^3/4$ x $33^1/4$	[25.4 x 95.3 x 844.6]	opening
1	front rail	1 x $1^1/8$ x $34^1/4$	[25.4 x 28.6 x 870]	$33^1/4$ [844.6] between tenons
2	mirror support uprights	$1^1/4$ x $1^3/4$ x $17^5/16$	[31.8 x 44.5 x 439.7]	
1	mirror support rail	1 x 3 x $29^3/4$	[25.4 x 76.2 x 755.6]	$28^3/4$ [730.3] between tenons
2	mirror frame stiles	$3/4$ x $1^1/2$ x $22^3/4$	[19.1 x 38.1 x 577.9]	
1	mirror frame bottom rail	$3/4$ x $1^1/2$ x $28^1/4$	[19.1 x 38.1 x 717.6]	
1	mirror frame arched top rail	$3/4$ x $1^1/2$ x $28^1/4$	[19.1 x 38.1 x 717.6]	bent to $79^1/4$ [2013] radius, or cut from $2^1/2$ [63.5] wide piece

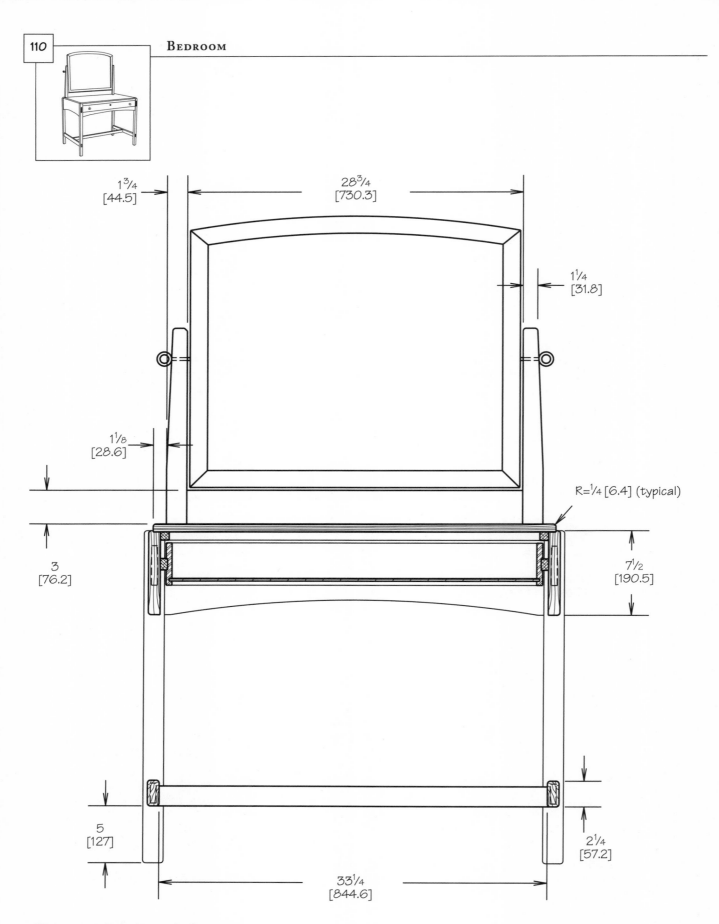

1³/₄
[44.5]

28³/₄
[730.3]

1¹/₄
[31.8]

1¹/₈
[28.6]

R=¹/₄ [6.4] (typical)

3
[76.2]

7¹/₂
[190.5]

5
[127]

2¹/₄
[57.2]

33¹/₄
[844.6]

Front section through drawer

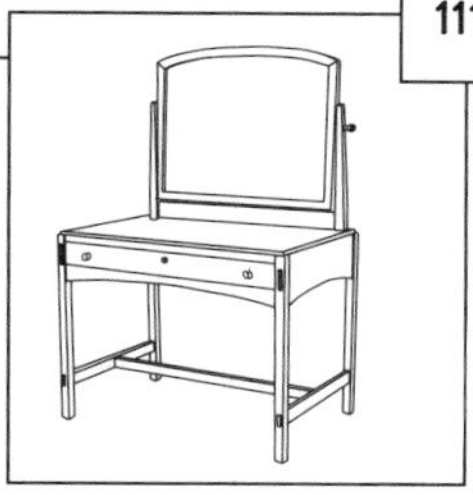

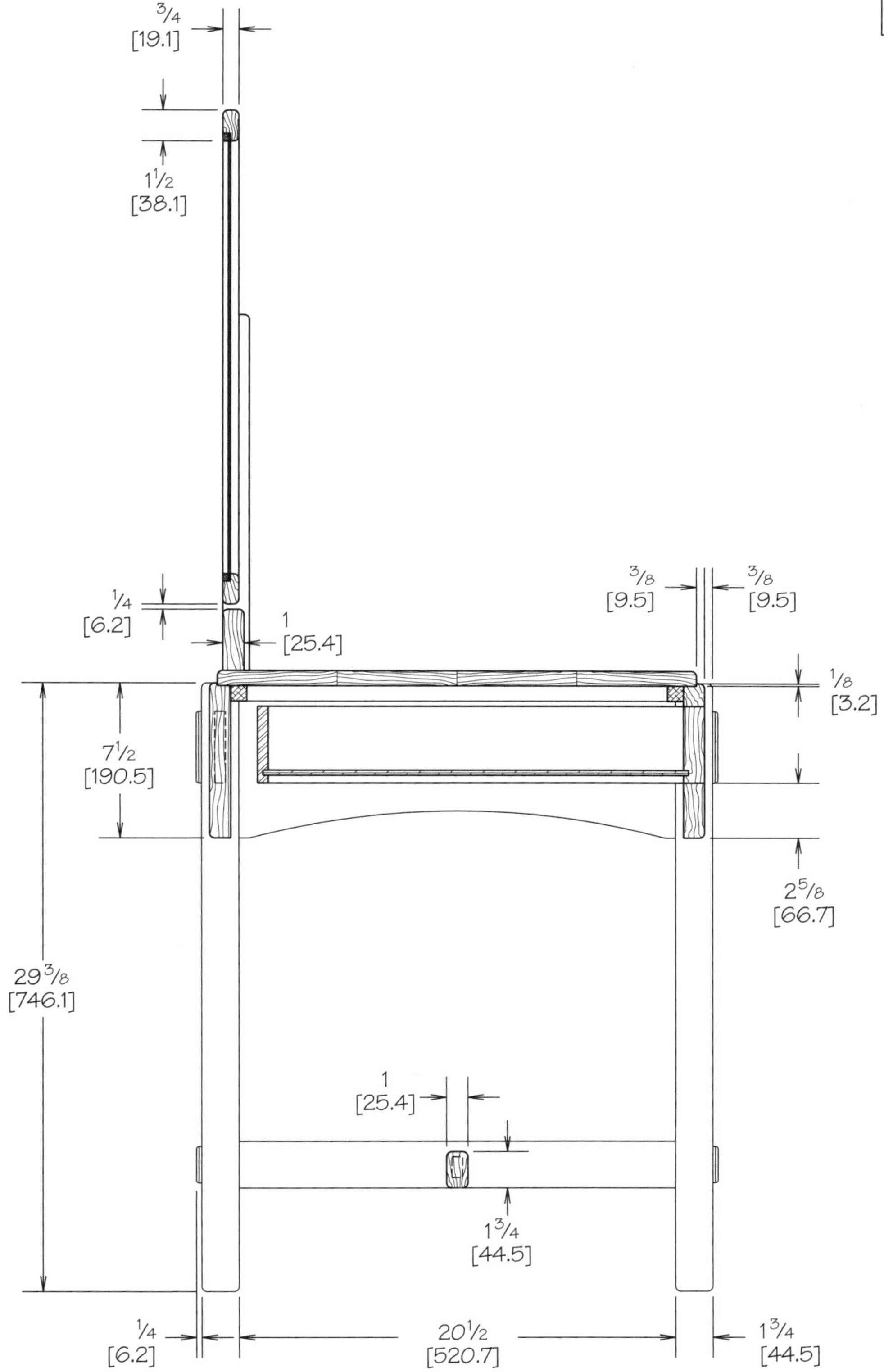

3/4
[19.1]

1 1/2
[38.1]

1/4
[6.2]

1
[25.4]

3/8
[9.5]

3/8
[9.5]

1/8
[3.2]

7 1/2
[190.5]

2 5/8
[66.7]

29 3/8
[746.1]

1
[25.4]

1 3/4
[44.5]

1/4
[6.2]

20 1/2
[520.7]

1 3/4
[44.5]

Side section through drawer

Top sits in ⅛ [3.2] deep
rabbet—attach top with screws in
oversized holes in cleats

¾ x ¾ [19.1 x 19.1]
cleats for
attaching top

1
[25.4]

³/₈
[9.5]

29³/₈
[746.1]

1³/₄
[44.5]

1³/₄
[44.5]

24
[609.6]

36
[914.4]

0   3   6   9   12
inches
[millimeters]

Assembly

L. & J. G. STICKLEY
NO. 110 NIGHTSTAND
29 x 14 x 18 [737 x 356 x 457]

Note that the arcs that form the feet at the bottom of the sides extend into the rails. The dimension given is to the line between the radii when the cut is finished. Make the bottom rail a little wider and cut the curves after the side panel is assembled. The arch in the apron under the drawers starts ½" in from the ends.

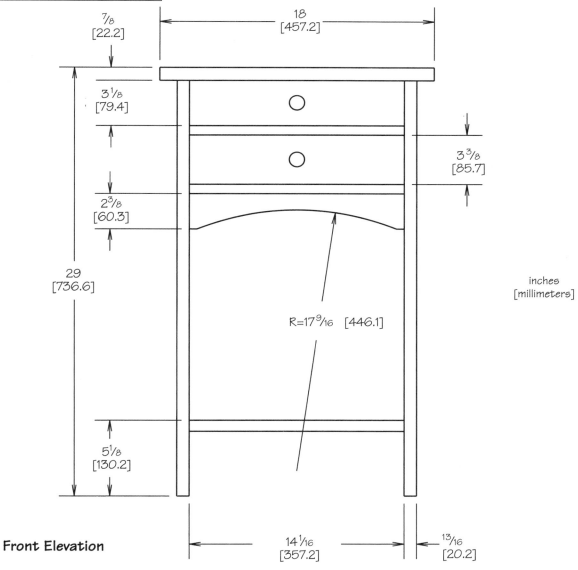

7/8
[22.2]

18
[457.2]

3 1/8
[79.4]

3 3/8
[85.7]

2 3/8
[60.3]

29
[736.6]

R=17 9/16 [446.1]

inches
[millimeters]

5 1/8
[130.2]

Front Elevation

14 1/16
[357.2]

13/16
[20.2]

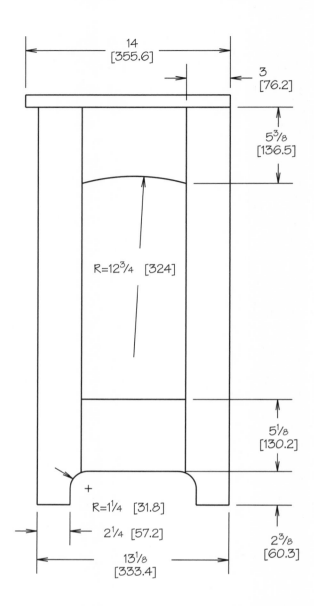

14
[355.6]

3
[76.2]

5³/₈
[136.5]

R=12³/₄   [324]

5¹/₈
[130.2]

+

R=1¹/₄   [31.8]

2¹/₄ [57.2]

2³/₈
[60.3]

13¹/₈
[333.4]

Side elevation

L. & J. G. Stickley No. 110 Nightstand

Qty	Part	Size		Notes
1	top	⁷/₈ x 14 x 18	[22.2 x 355.6 x 457.2]	
2	sides	¹³/₁₆ x 13¹/₈ x 28¹/₈	[20.6 x 333.4 x 714.4]	assembled-parts detailed below
4	stiles	¹³/₁₆ x 3 x 28¹/₈	[20.6 x 76.2 x 714.4]	
2	bottom rails	¹³/₁₆ x 5¹/₈ x 8¹/₈	[20.6 x 130.2 x 206.4]	7¹/₈ [181.0] between tenons
2	top rails	¹³/₁₆ x 5³/₈ x 8¹/₈	[20.6 x 136.5 x 206.4]	7¹/₈ [181.0] between tenons
1	bottom shelf	¹³/₁₆ x 12¹/₈ x 14¹³/₁₆	[20.6 x 308 x 376.2]	14¹/₁₆ [357.2] between tenons
1	back	³/₄ x 7³/₄ x 14¹³/₁₆	[19.1 x 196.9 x 376.2]	14¹/₁₆ [357.2] between tenons
1	arched apron	³/₄ x 2³/₈ x 14¹³/₁₆	[19.1 x 60.3 x 376.2]	14¹/₁₆ [357.2] between tenons
2	rails	⁵/₈ x 3 x 14¹³/₁₆	[15.9 x 76.2 x 376.2]	14¹/₁₆ [357.2] between tenons
1	bottom drawer front	³/₄ x 3³/₈ x 14¹/₁₆	[19.1 x 85.7 x 357.2]	opening
1	top drawer front	³/₄ x 3¹/₈ x 14¹/₁₆	[19.1 x 79.4 x 357.2]	opening
1	panel	¹/₄ x 7⁷/₈ x 16¹/₂	[6.4 x 200 x 419.1]	7¹/₈ [181] x 15³/₄ [400] exposed

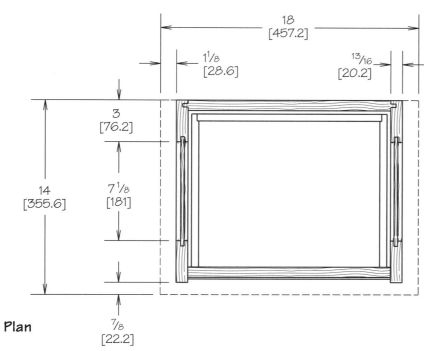

18
[457.2]

1 1/8
[28.6]

13/16
[20.2]

3
[76.2]

14
[355.6]

7 1/8
[181]

Plan

7/8
[22.2]

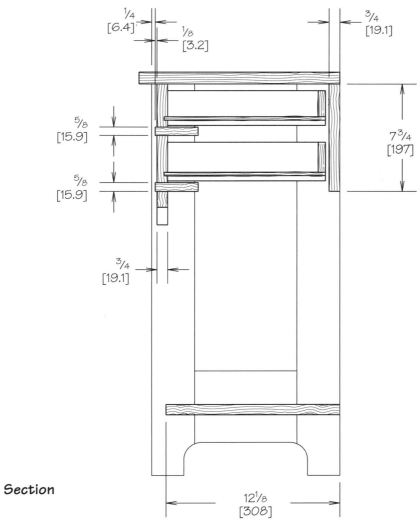

1/4
[6.4]

1/8
[3.2]

3/4
[19.1]

5/8
[15.9]

7 3/4
[197]

5/8
[15.9]

3/4
[19.1]

Section

12 1/8
[308]

LIBRARY AND DEN

No. 74 Bookrack with
Keyed Tenons 118

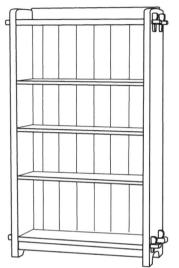

No. 644 Open Bookcase 120

No. 72 Harvey Ellis
Magazine Cabinet   123

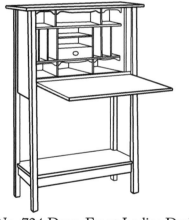

No. 724 Drop-Front Ladies Desk   126

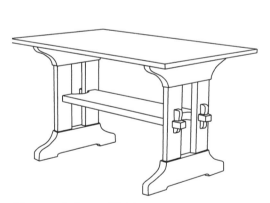

No.637 Library Table 131

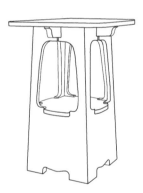

Limbert Lamp Table 141

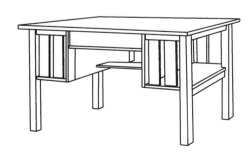

No. 503 Desk with Bookcase Ends 134

No. 616 Library Table with 2 Drawers 138

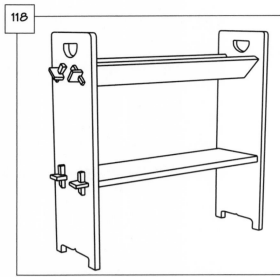

GUSTAV STICKLEY
NO. 74 BOOKCASE
31 high x 30 wide x 10 deep [787 x 762 x 254]

Practice making keyed mortise and tenon joints with this small piece. The angled top shelf is good for easy access to reference books, without having to bend over to see the titles.

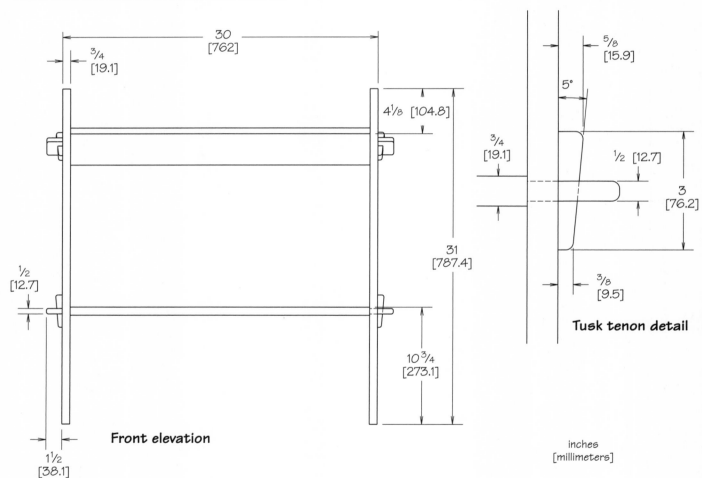

Front elevation

Tusk tenon detail

inches
[millimeters]

Gustav Stickley No. 74 Bookcase

QTY	PART	SIZE		NOTES
2	sides	³⁄₄ x 10 x 31	[19.1 x 254 x 787.4]	
2	top shelves	³⁄₄ x 4 x 33	[19.1 x 101.6 x 838.2]	28¹⁄₂ [723.9] between tenons
1	bottom shelf	³⁄₄ x 8 x 33	[19.1 x 203.2 x 838.2]	28¹⁄₂ [723.9] between tenons
8	keys	³⁄₄ x ⁵⁄₈ x 3	[19.1 x 15.9 x 76.2]	

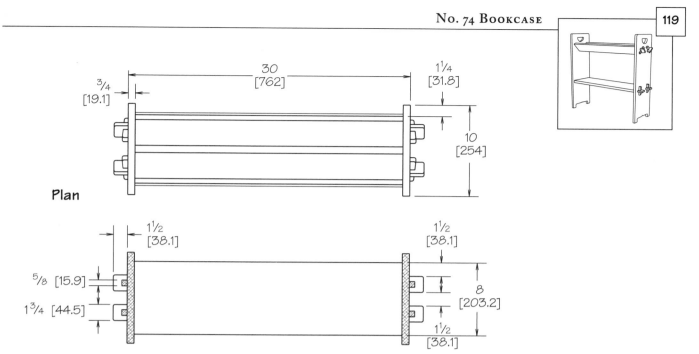

Plan

Plan section at shelf

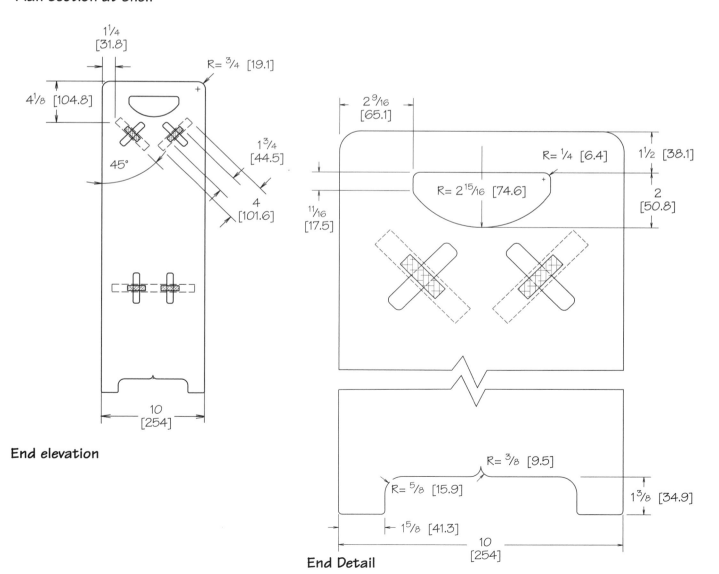

End elevation

End Detail

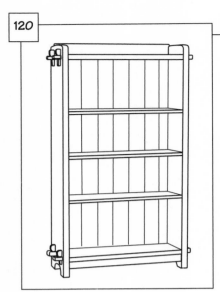

L. & J. G. STICKLEY No. 644 BOOKCASE
55 high x 36 wide x 12 deep [1397 x 915 x 305]

This bookcase was made in several widths, 30" [762], 36" [915], 49" [1247] and 70" [1778] wide. It could easily be made any width desired. The widest version had two vertical dividers, but the sides and basic construction of all four versions was the same. The shelves could be made fixed, but the rest of the structure is so stout that there is no reason not to have them be adjustable. Gustav Stickley made bookcases very similar to this, but the sides were not as thick as in this example.

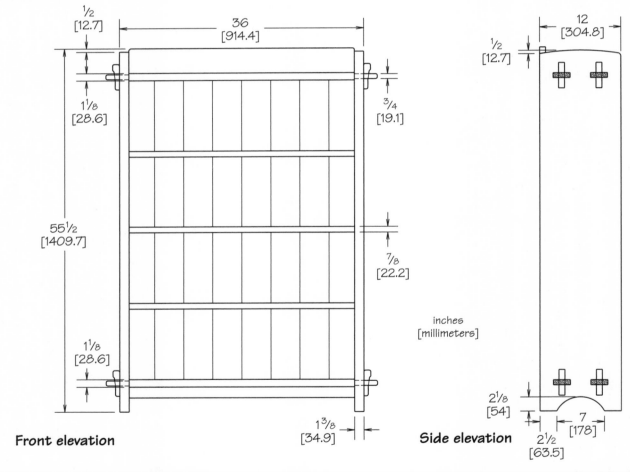

Front elevation

Side elevation

L. & J. G. Stickley No. 644 Bookcase

QTY	PART	SIZE		NOTES
2	Sides	1³⁄₈ x 12 x 55	[34.9 x 304.8 x 1397]	
2	Top & Bottom	1¹⁄₈ x 12 x 40	[28.6 x 304.8 x 1016]	33¹⁄₄ [344.6] between tenons
3	Shelves	⁷⁄₈ x 11 x 33¹⁄₄	[22.2 x 279.4 x 844.6]	opening
8	Back Planks	³⁄₄ x 4⁵⁄₁₆ x 46³⁄₄	[19.1 x 109.5 x 1187.5]	
8	Keys	⁷⁄₈ x 1 x 3⁷⁄₈	[22.2 x 25.4 x 98.4]	
1	Backsplash	⁷⁄₈ x 3³⁄₄ x 33¹⁄₄	[22.2 x 95.3 x 844.6	

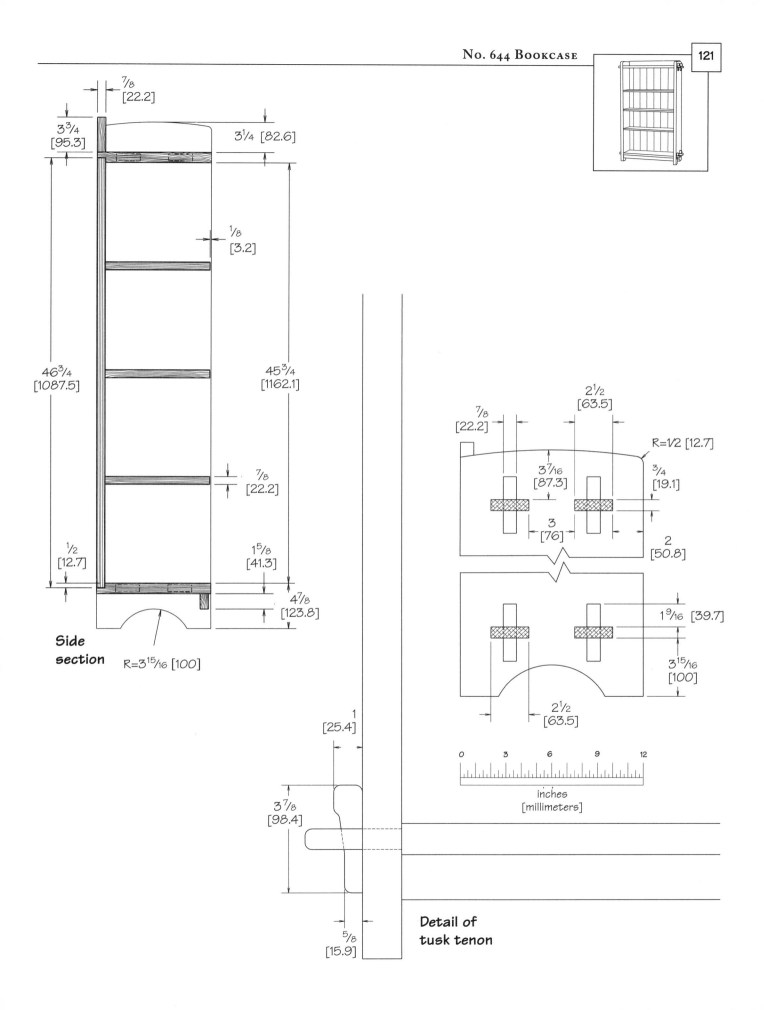

7/8
[22.2]

3 3/4
[95.3]

3 1/4 [82.6]

1/8
[3.2]

46 3/4
[1087.5]

45 3/4
[1162.1]

7/8
[22.2]

1/2
[12.7]

1 5/8
[41.3]

4 7/8
[123.8]

**Side
section**

R=3 15/16 [100]

1
[25.4]

3 7/8
[98.4]

5/8
[15.9]

**Detail of
tusk tenon**

7/8
[22.2]

2 1/2
[63.5]

R=1/2 [12.7]

3 7/16
[87.3]

3/4
[19.1]

3
[76]

2
[50.8]

1 9/16 [39.7]

3 15/16
[100]

2 1/2
[63.5]

0   3   6   9   12

inches
[millimeters]

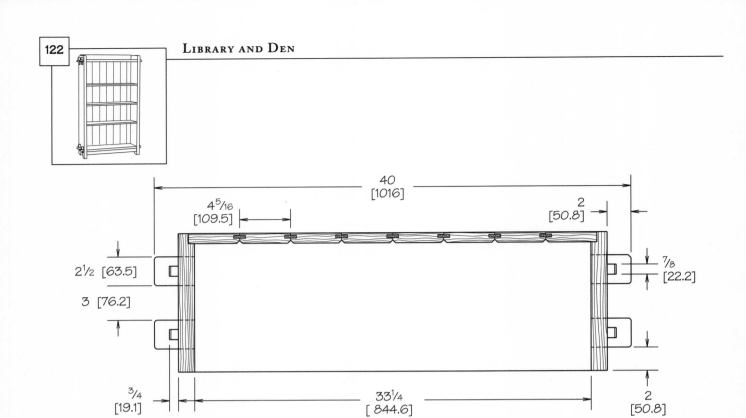

Plan section above top shelf

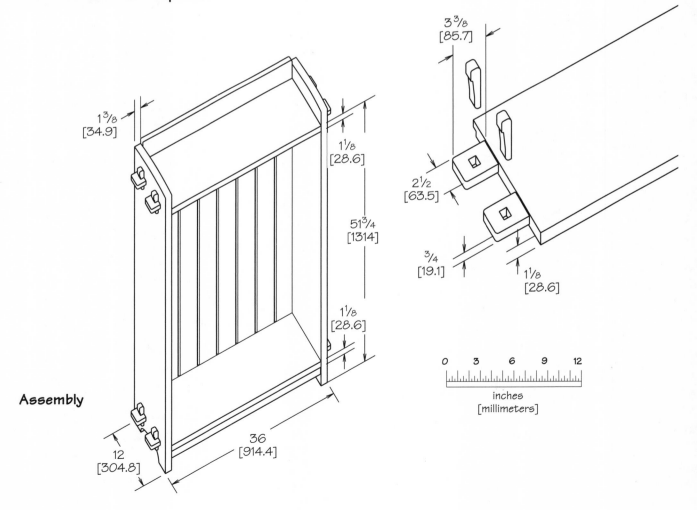

Assembly

Gustav Stickley
No. 72 Magazine Cabinet

42 x 22 x 13 [1067 x 559 x 330]

An excellent example of Harvey Ellis' design motifs. Note that the shelves are dadoed only into the side panels, not the legs. This simplifies the construction by reducing the number of mortises to cut into the legs (although it does make the shelves a little trickier). Assemble each side as a unit, then assemble the shelves and stretchers. The top goes on last, held down by table irons.

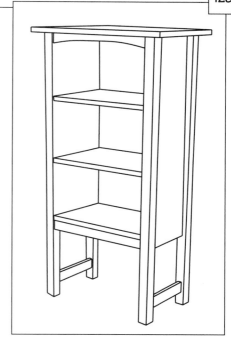

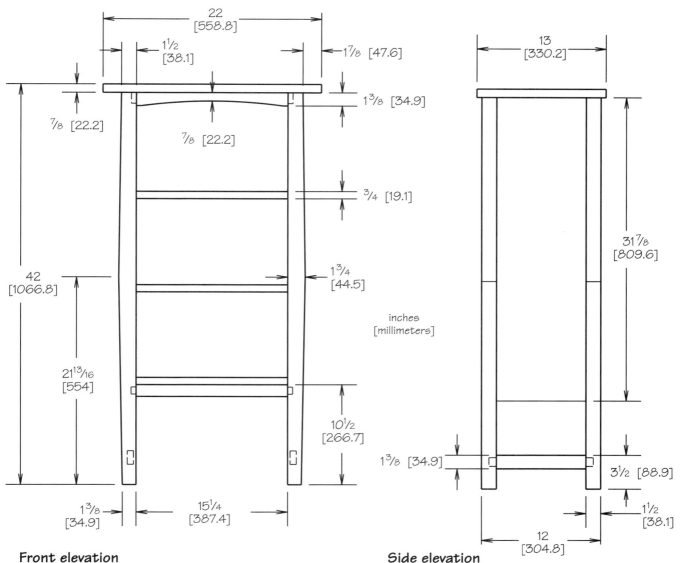

inches
[millimeters]

Front elevation

Side elevation

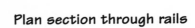

Plan section through rails

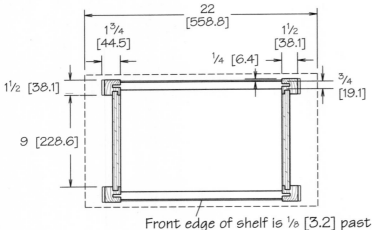

22 [558.8]

1³/₄ [44.5]   1¹/₂ [38.1]   ¹/₄ [6.4]   ³/₄ [19.1]

1¹/₂ [38.1]

9 [228.6]

Front edge of shelf is ¹/₈ [3.2] past rail,
¹/₈ [3.2] behind front of leg

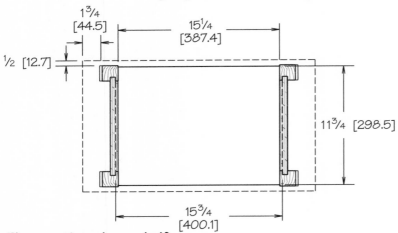

1³/₄ [44.5]   15¹/₄ [387.4]

¹/₂ [12.7]

11³/₄ [298.5]

15³/₄ [400.1]

Plan section above shelf

0   3   6   9   12

inches
[millimeters]

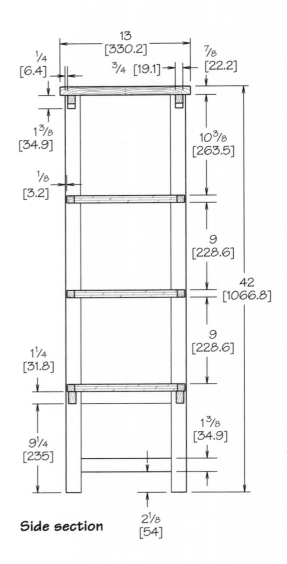

13 [330.2]   ⁷/₈ [22.2]

¹/₄ [6.4]   ³/₄ [19.1]

1³/₈ [34.9]

10³/₈ [263.5]

¹/₈ [3.2]

9 [228.6]

42 [1066.8]

9 [228.6]

1¹/₄ [31.8]

1³/₈ [34.9]

9¹/₄ [235]

Side section

2¹/₈ [54]

Gustav Stickley No. 72 Magazine Cabinet

QTY	PART	SIZE		NOTES
4	legs	1¹/₂ x 1³/₄ x 41¹/₈	[38.1 x 44.5 x 1044.6]	
2	side stretchers	⁵/₈ x 1³/₈ x 10¹/₂	[15.9 x 34.9 x 266.7]	9 [228.6] between tenons
2	side panels	³/₄ x 9³/₄ x 31⁷/₈	[19.1 x 247.7 x 809.6]	9 [228.6] between tenons
2	rails below bottom shelf	³/₄ x 1¹/₄ x 16³/₄	[19.1 x 31.8 x 425.5]	15¹/₄ [387.4] between tenons
2	arched rails below top	³/₄ x 1³/₈ 16³/₄	[19.1 x 34.9 x 425.5]	15¹/₄ [387.4] between tenons
3	shelves	³/₄ x 11³/₄ x 15³/₄	[19.1 x 298.5 x 400.1]	15¹/₄ [387.4] exposed
1	top	⁷/₈ x 13 x 22	[22.2 x 330.2 x 558.8]	

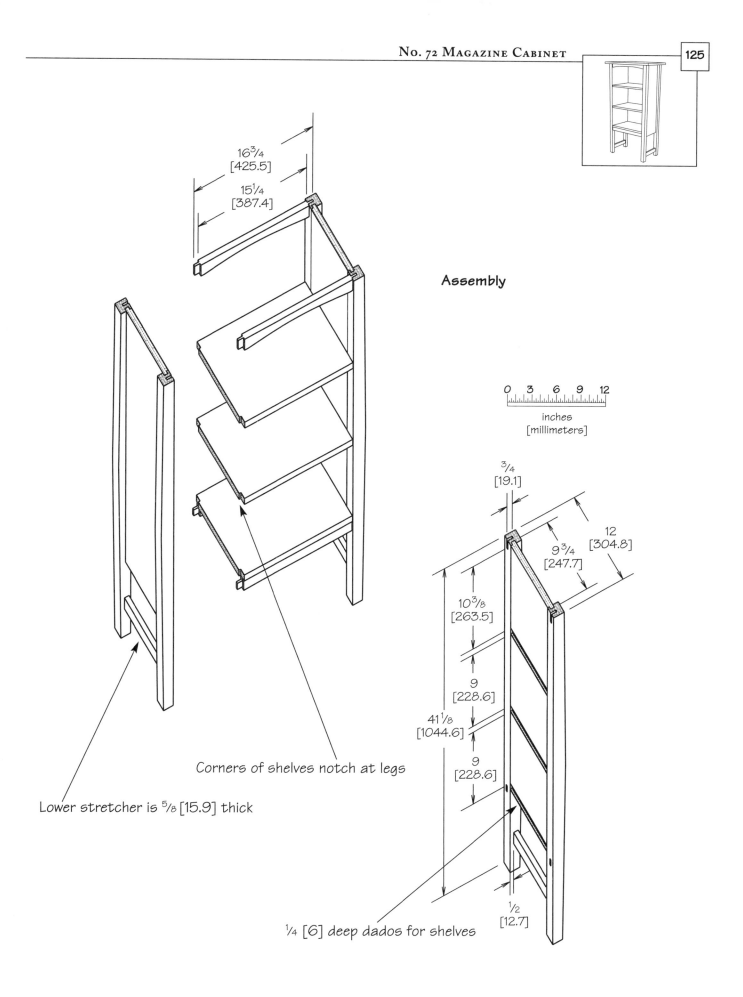

16³⁄₄ [425.5]

15¹⁄₄ [387.4]

Assembly

0 3 6 9 12
inches [millimeters]

³⁄₄ [19.1]

9³⁄₄ [247.7]

12 [304.8]

10³⁄₈ [263.5]

9 [228.6]

41¹⁄₈ [1044.6]

9 [228.6]

Lower stretcher is ⁵⁄₈ [15.9] thick

Corners of shelves notch at legs

¹⁄₄ [6] deep dados for shelves

¹⁄₂ [12.7]

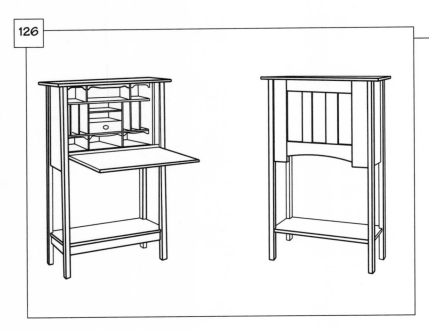

GUSTAV STICKLEY
NO. 724
LADIES' BOOKCASE
46 high x 32 wide x 12 deep
[1168 x 813 x 305]

The prototype of this small desk had flori-
form inlays on the narrow front panels. The
inlaid furniture never went into full production, but this handsome little desk was produced as shown for several years. Make the
pigeonholes as a separate unit, and attach
that inside the upper case.

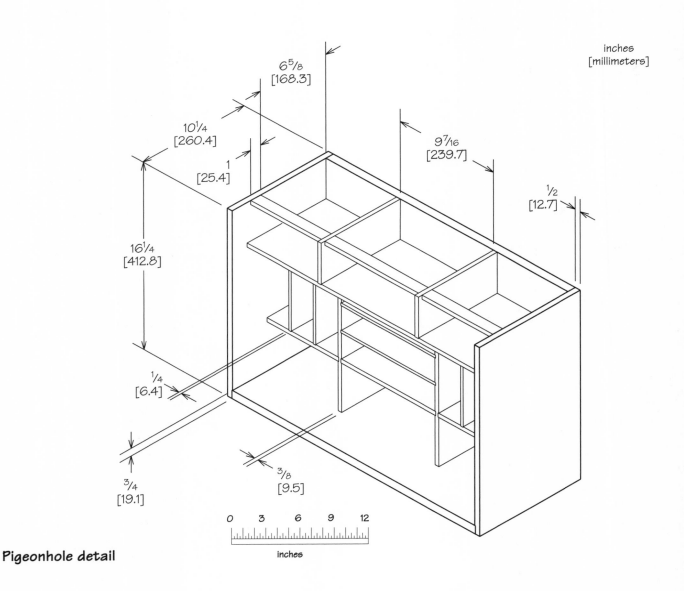

Pigeonhole detail

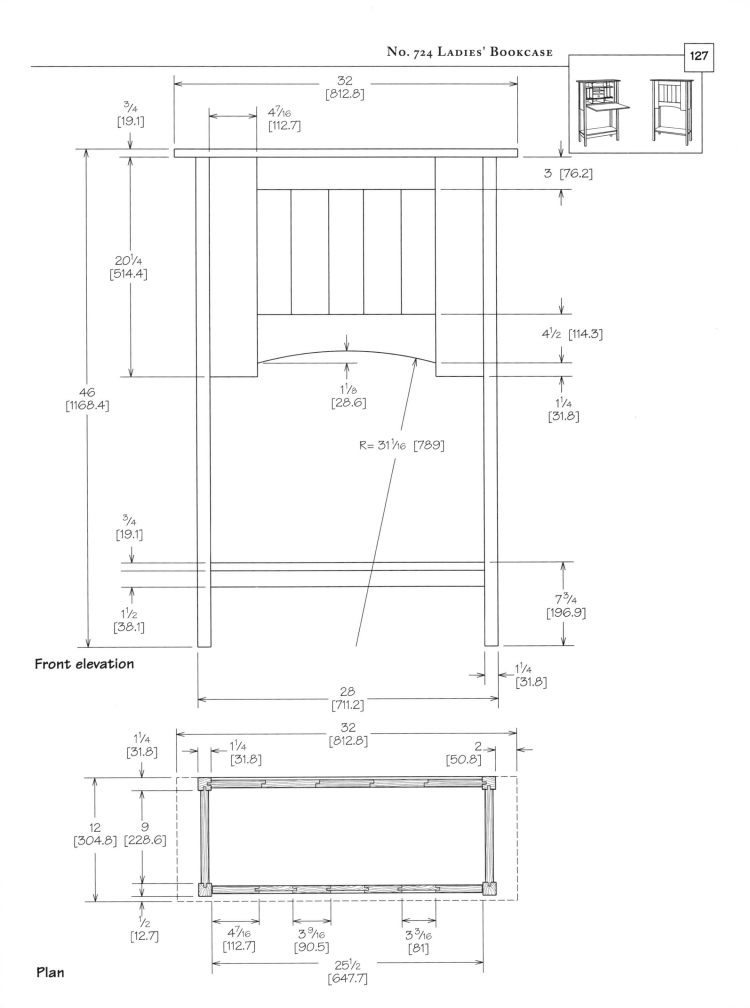

32
[812.8]

3/4
[19.1]

4⁷/16
[112.7]

3 [76.2]

20¹/4
[514.4]

4¹/2 [114.3]

1¹/4
[31.8]

1¹/8
[28.6]

R= 31¹/16 [789]

46
[1168.4]

3/4
[19.1]

7³/4
[196.9]

1¹/2
[38.1]

Front elevation

28
[711.2]

1¹/4
[31.8]

32
[812.8]

1¹/4
[31.8]

1¹/4
[31.8]

2
[50.8]

12
[304.8]

9
[228.6]

1/2
[12.7]

4⁷/16
[112.7]

3⁹/16
[90.5]

3³/16
[81]

25¹/2
[647.7]

Plan

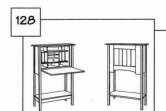

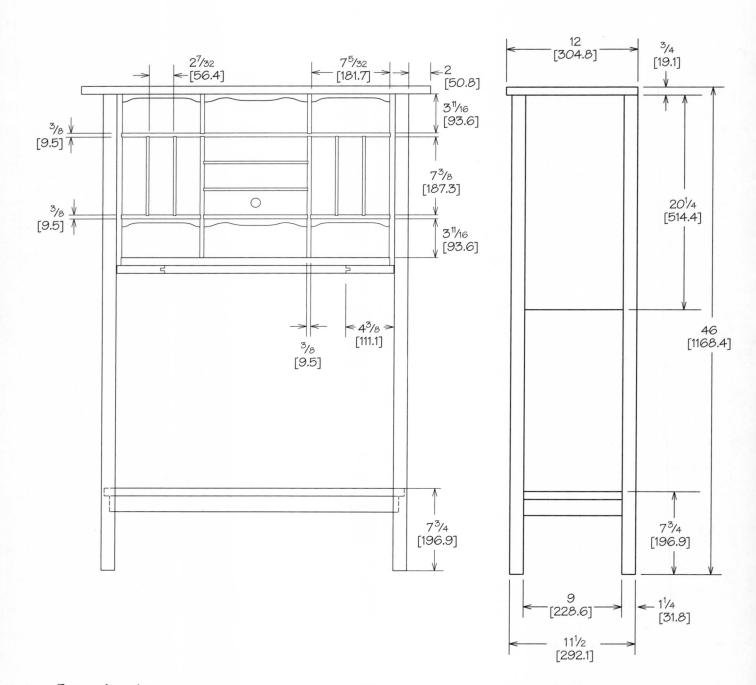

Front elevation - open

Side elevation

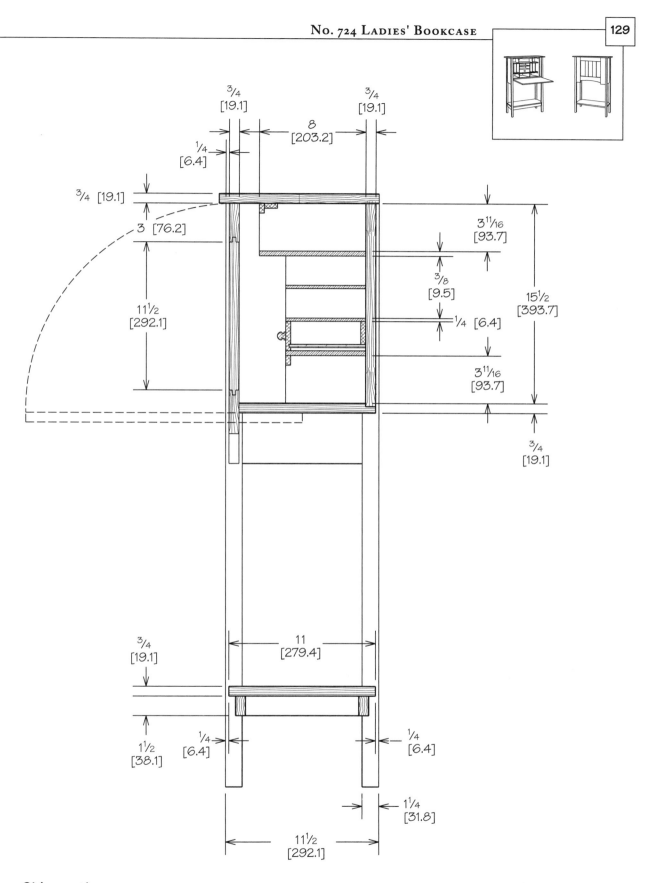

$^3/_4$
[19.1]

$^3/_4$
[19.1]

8
[203.2]

$^1/_4$
[6.4]

$^3/_4$ [19.1]

3 [76.2]

$3^{11}/_{16}$
[93.7]

$^3/_8$
[9.5]

$^1/_4$ [6.4]

$15^1/_2$
[393.7]

$11^1/_2$
[292.1]

$3^{11}/_{16}$
[93.7]

$^3/_4$
[19.1]

11
[279.4]

$^3/_4$
[19.1]

$^1/_4$
[6.4]

$^1/_4$
[6.4]

$1^1/_2$
[38.1]

$1^1/_4$
[31.8]

$11^1/_2$
[292.1]

Side section

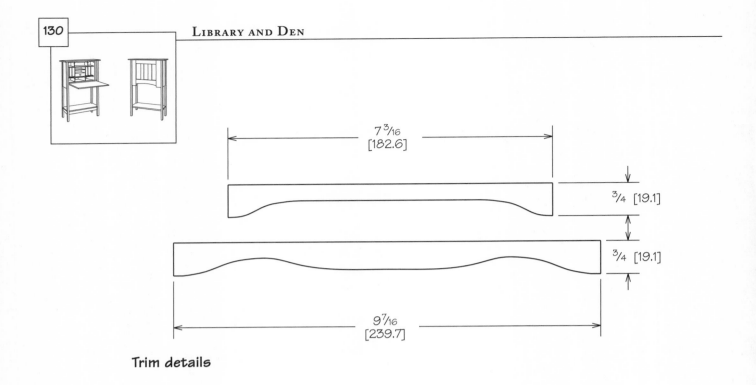

7³/₁₆ [182.6]

³/₄ [19.1]

³/₄ [19.1]

9⁷/₁₆ [239.7]

Trim details

Gustav Stickley No. 724 Ladies' Bookcase

QTY	PART	SIZE		NOTES
4	legs	1¼ x 1¼ x 45¼	[31.8 x 31.8 x 1149.4]	
1	top	³/₄ x 12 x 32	[19.1 x 304.8 x 812.8]	
2	front & back shelf rails	³/₄ x 1½ x 26½	[19.1 x 38.1 x 673.1]	
2	shelf end rails	³/₄ x 1½ x 10	[19.1 x 38.1 x 254]	
1	lower shelf	³/₄ x 11 x 27½	[19.1 x 279.4 x 698.5]	
2	side panels	³/₄ x 10 x 20¼	[19.1 x 254 x 514.4]	9 [228.6] between tenons
1	door	³/₄ x 25½ x 20¼	[19.1 x 644.7 x 514.4]	opening—parts detailed below
2	stiles	³/₄ x 4⁷/₁₆ x 20¼	[19.1 x 112.7 x 447.7]	
1	bottom door rail	³/₄ x 4½ x 17⁵/₈	[19.1 x 114.3 x 447.7]	16⁵/₈ [422.3] between tenons
1	top door rail	³/₄ x 3 x 17⁵/₈	[19.1 x 76.2 x 447.7]	16⁵/₈ [422.3] between tenons
2	inner door stiles	³/₄ x 3⁹/₁₆ x 12½	[19.1 x 90.5 x 317.5]	11½ [292.1] between tenons
3	door panels	½ x 4⁹/₁₆ x 12½	[12.7 x 115.9 x 317.5]	3⁹/₁₆ x 11½ [90.5 x 292.1] exposed
1	cabinet bottom	³/₄ x 10¼ x 24	[19.1 x 260.4 x 609.6]	
1	cabinet back	³/₄ x 15³/₄ x 25½	[19.1 x 400.1 x 647.7]	
2	cabinet sides	³/₄ x 10¼ x 17	[19.1 x 260.4 x 431.8]	
1	cabinet shelf	³/₈ x 8 x 24	[9.5 x 203.2 x 609.6]	
2	vertical dividers	³/₈ x 6 x 11½	[9.5 x 152.4 x 292.1]	
2	upper vertical dividers	³/₈ x 8 x 3³/₄	[9.5 x 203.2 x 95.3]	
1	shelf	³/₈ x 8 x 24⁵/₈	[9.5 x 203.2 x 625.5]	
2	shelves	³/₈ x 6 x 7⁹/₃₂	[9.5 x 152.4 x 184.9]	
1	shelf	³/₈ x 6 x 9⁹/₁₆	[9.5 x 152.4 x 242.9]	
2	shelves	¼ x 6 x 9⁹/₁₆	[6.4 x 152.4 x 242.9]	
4	vertical dividers	¼ x 6 x 7½	[6.4 x 152.4 x 190.5]	
1	drawer front	³/₈ x 2⁹/₁₆ x 9⁷/₁₆	[9.5 x 65.1 x 240.0]	opening
2	center curved trim	³/₈ x ³/₄ x 9⁷/₁₆	[9.5 x 19.1 x 240.0]	
4	outer curved trim	³/₈ x ³/₄ x 7⁵/₃₂	[9.5 x 19.1 x 181.8]	

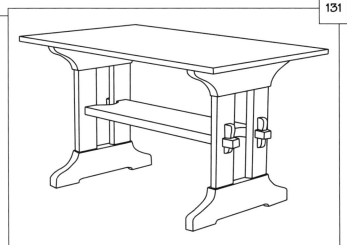

NO. 637 LIBRARY TABLE

29 high x 30 wide x 48 long [737 x 762 x 1219]

Here is a robust library table that could be used as a computer desk, a conference table, or a dining table. It would be easy to adjust the length and width to your particular purpose. The keyed tenons make an especially attractive detail.

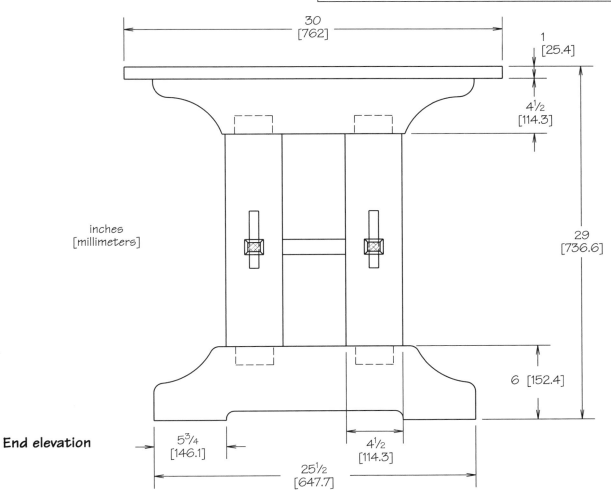

inches [millimeters]

End elevation

Gustav Stickley No. 637 Library Table

QTY	PART	SIZE		NOTES
2	feet	1³/₄ x 6 x 25¹/₂	[44.5 x 152.4 x 647.7]	
2	top rails	1³/₄ x 4¹/₂ x 25¹/₂	[44.5 x 114.3 x 647.7]	
4	uprights	1¹/₄ x 4¹/₂ x 21¹/₂	[31.8 x 114.3 x 546.1]	18¹/₂ [470.0] between tenons
1	shelf	1¹/₄ x 14 x 41	[31.8 x 355.6 x 1041.4]	33¹/₂ [825.5] between tenons
1	top	1 x 30 x 48	[25.4 x 762 x 1219.2]	
4	keys	³/₄ x 1⁷/₁₆ x 4³/₄	[19.1 x 36.5 x 120.7]	

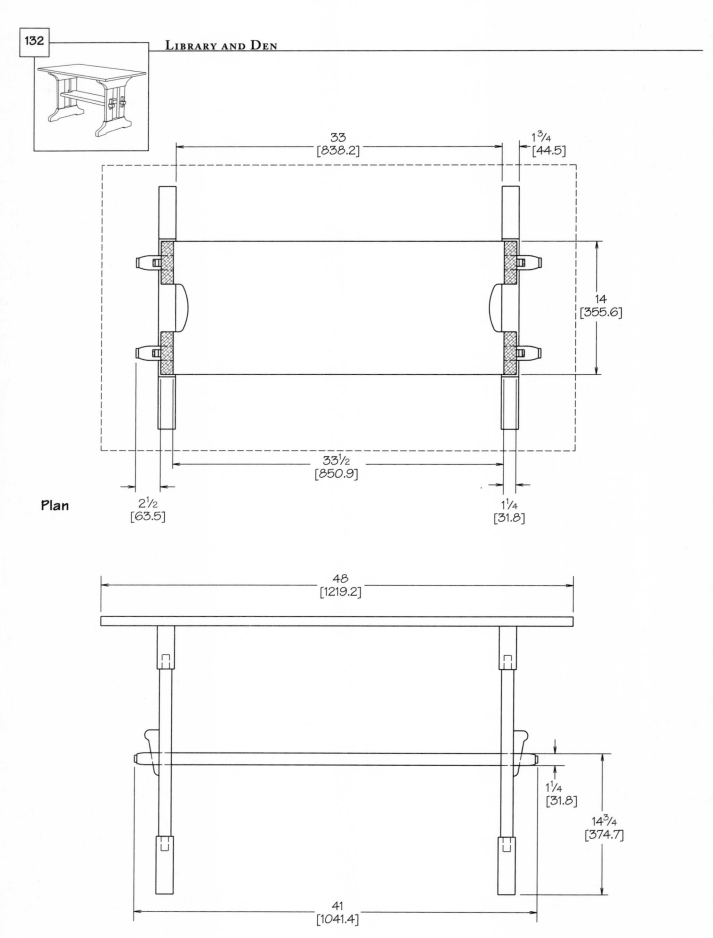

33
[838.2]

1³/₄
[44.5]

14
[355.6]

33¹/₂
[850.9]

Plan

2¹/₂
[63.5]

1¹/₄
[31.8]

48
[1219.2]

1¹/₄
[31.8]

14³/₄
[374.7]

41
[1041.4]

Front elevation

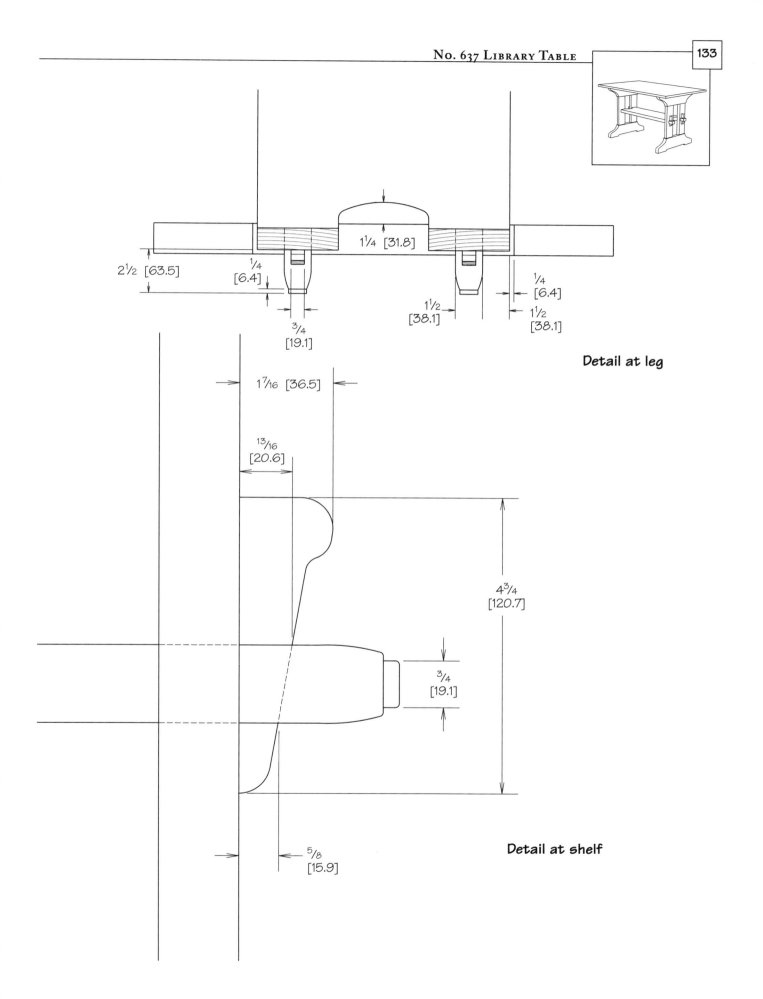

1¼ [31.8]

2½ [63.5]

¼ [6.4]

¼ [6.4]

1½ [38.1]

1½ [38.1]

¾ [19.1]

Detail at leg

1⁷⁄₁₆ [36.5]

¹³⁄₁₆ [20.6]

4¾ [120.7]

¾ [19.1]

⅝ [15.9]

Detail at shelf

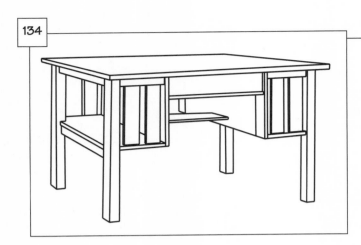

GUSTAV STICKLEY
NO. 503 DESK
42 x 28 x 30 [1067 x 711 x 762]

With drawers on opposite sides, this can be used as a partner's desk. If placing against a wall, eliminate the back drawer, and substitute a solid panel. The drawer could easily be replaced with a pull-out tray for a computer keyboard, or for a lap-top computer.

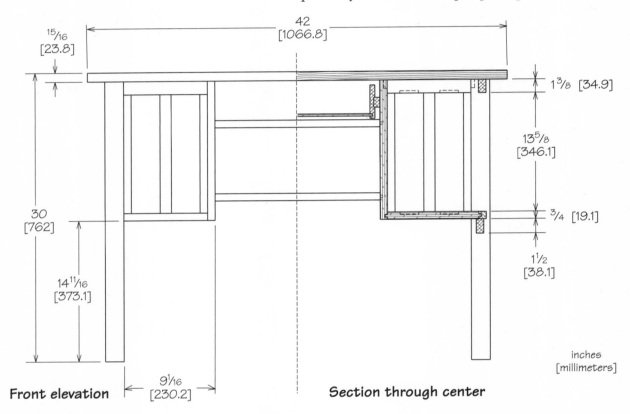

Front elevation

Section through center

inches
[millimeters]

Gustav Stickley No. 503 Desk

Qty	Part	Size		Notes
4	legs	1⁷/₈ x 1⁷/₈ x 29¹/₁₆	[47.6 x 47.6 x 738.2]	
1	top	¹⁵/₁₆ x 28 x 42	[23.8 x 711.2 x 1066.8]	
2	shelves	³/₄ x 10¹/₈ x 23¹/₂	[19.1 x 257.2 x 596.9]	plywood with solid wood edges
2	backs	³/₄ x 15³/₄ x 17¹/₂	[19.1 x 400.1 x 444.5]	plywood
4	back edges	³/₄ x 3 x 15³/₄	[19.1 x 76.2 x 400.1]	
1	stretcher	³/₄ x 4¹/₄ x 17¹/₄	[19.1 x 108 x 438.2]	
4	bookshelf side rails	³/₄ x 1³/₈ x 9¹/₈	[19.1 x 34.9 x 231.8]	8³/₈ [212.7] between tenons
2	bookshelf end rails	³/₄ x 1³/₈ x 21¹/₂	[19.1 x 34.9 x 546.1]	20³/₄ [527.1] between tenons
2	bookshelf bottom rails	³/₄ x 1¹/₂ x 21¹/₂	[19.1 x 38.1 x 546.1]	20³/₄ [527.1]between tenons
1	shelf below drawers	³/₄ x 23 x 16¹/₂	[19.1 x 584.2 x 419.1]	plywood with solid wood edges
2	drawer rails	³/₄ x 3¹/₂ x 16¹/₂	[19.1 x 88.9 x 419.1]	
8	shelf slats	¹/₂ x 2⁷/₈ x 13	[12.7 x 73 x 330.2]	12¹/₄ [311.2] between tenons
2	drawer fronts	³/₄ x 4¹/₁₆ x 16¹/₂	[19.1 x 103.2 x 419.1]	opening size

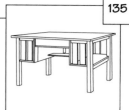

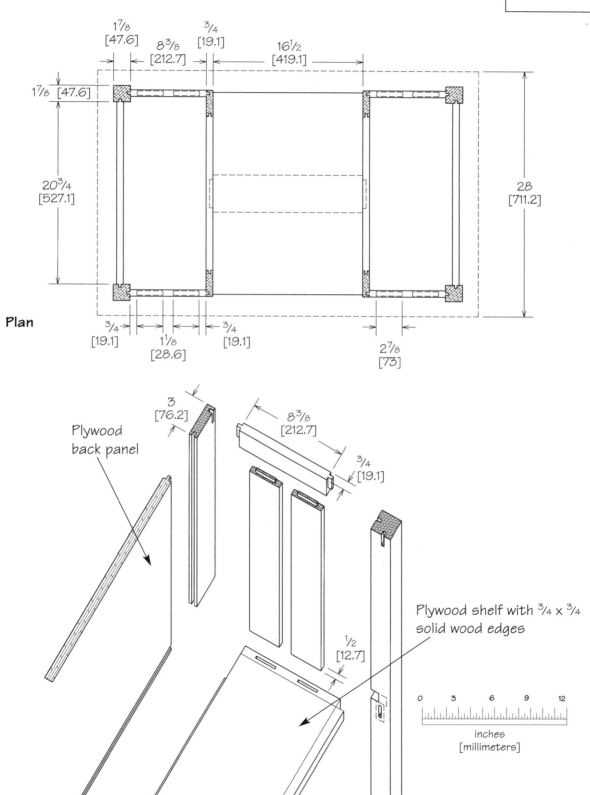

$1\frac{7}{8}$ [47.6]

$8\frac{3}{8}$ [212.7]

$\frac{3}{4}$ [19.1]

$16\frac{1}{2}$ [419.1]

$1\frac{7}{8}$ [47.6]

$20\frac{3}{4}$ [527.1]

28 [711.2]

Plan

$\frac{3}{4}$ [19.1]

$1\frac{1}{8}$ [28.6]

$\frac{3}{4}$ [19.1]

$2\frac{7}{8}$ [73]

3 [76.2]

$8\frac{3}{8}$ [212.7]

$\frac{3}{4}$ [19.1]

Plywood back panel

Plywood shelf with $\frac{3}{4}$ x $\frac{3}{4}$ solid wood edges

$\frac{1}{2}$ [12.7]

0   3   6   9   12

inches [millimeters]

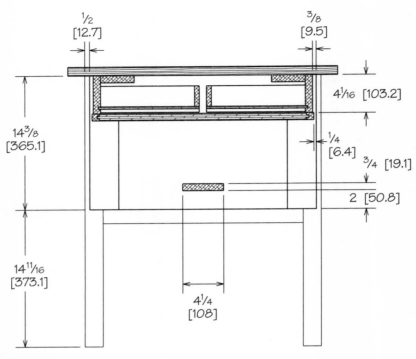

1/2 [12.7]

3/8 [9.5]

4 1/16 [103.2]

14 3/8 [365.1]

1/4 [6.4]

3/4 [19.1]

2 [50.8]

14 11/16 [373.1]

4 1/4 [108]

Section through center

0 3 6 9 12

inches [millimeters]

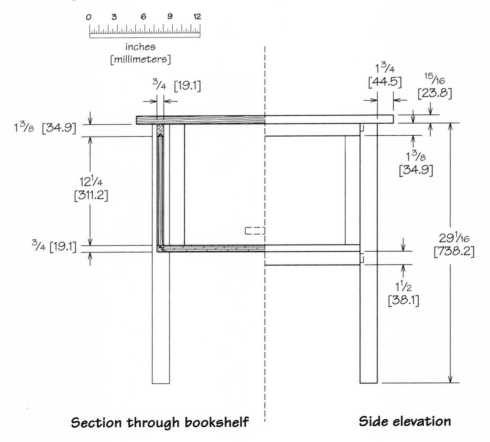

3/4 [19.1]

1 3/4 [44.5]

15/16 [23.8]

1 3/8 [34.9]

1 3/8 [34.9]

12 1/4 [311.2]

29 1/16 [738.2]

3/4 [19.1]

1 1/2 [38.1]

Section through bookshelf   **Side elevation**

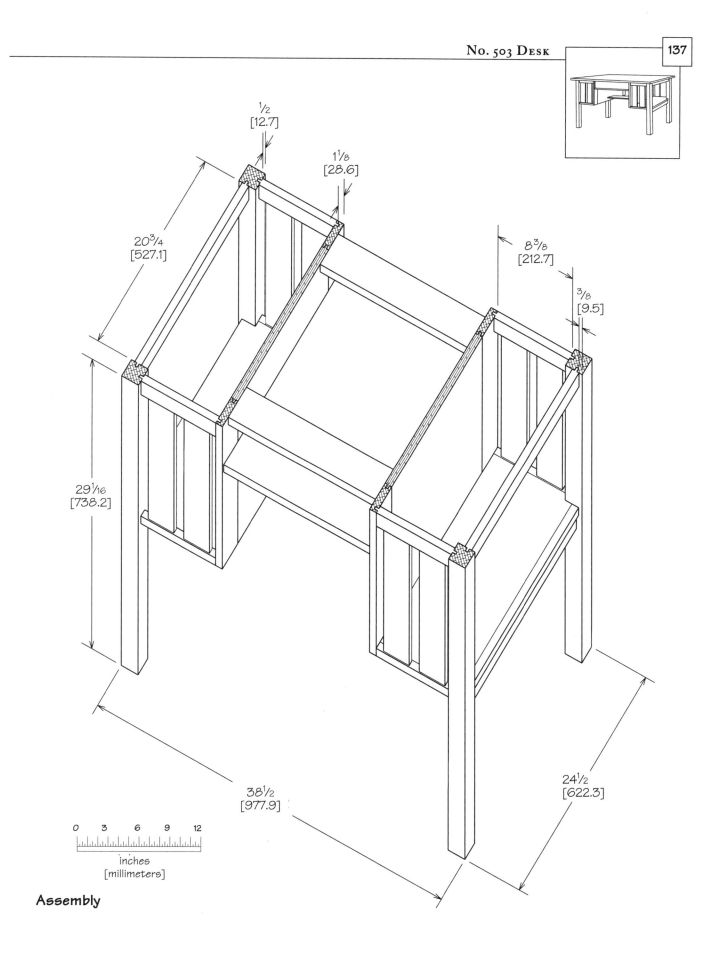

½
[12.7]

1⅛
[28.6]

20¾
[527.1]

8⅜
[212.7]

3/8
[9.5]

29 1/16
[738.2]

24½
[622.3]

38½
[977.9]

0 3 6 9 12

inches
[millimeters]

Assembly

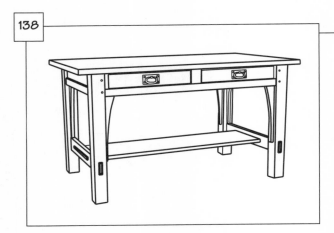

GUSTAV STICKLEY
NO. 616 LIBRARY TABLE
30 high x 32 deep x 54 wide [762 x 813 x 1372]

Many variations of this table were made—it was available with a leather top or a wooden top, and appeared in some catalogs with three drawers instead of two as shown in this example. Similar tables were also manufactured in different sizes with different model numbers.

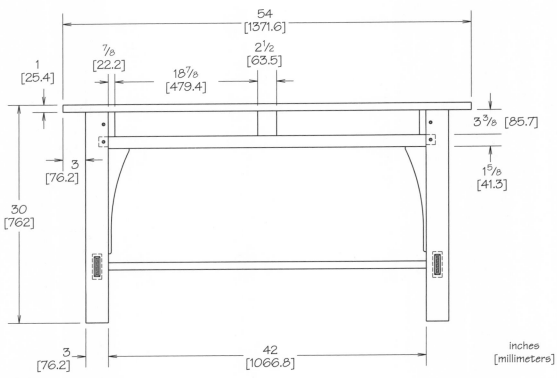

Front elevation

Gustav Stickley No. 616 Library Table

QTY	PART	SIZE		NOTES
1	top	1 x 32 x 54	[25.4 x 812.8 x 1371.6]	
4	Legs	3 x 3 x 29	[76.2 x 76.2 x 736.6]	
2	lower rails	$1\frac{1}{4}$ x $3\frac{1}{2}$ x $30\frac{3}{4}$	[31.8 x 88.9 x 781.1]	24 [609.6] between tenons
2	upper rails	$1\frac{1}{2}$ x $1\frac{5}{8}$ x $26\frac{1}{2}$	[38.1 x 41.3 x 673.1]	24 [609.6] between tenons
2	panels below top	$\frac{3}{4}$ x $3\frac{3}{8}$ x $26\frac{1}{2}$	[19.1 x 85.7 x 673.1]	24 [609.6] between tenons
1	shelf	1 x $13\frac{3}{4}$ x $46\frac{7}{8}$	[25.4 x 349.2 x 1190.6]	$43\frac{5}{8}$ [1108.1]between tenons
2	front & back rails	$1\frac{1}{2}$ x $1\frac{5}{8}$ x $43\frac{1}{2}$	[38.1 x 41.3 x 1104.9]	42 [1066.8] between tenons
1	back panel below top	$\frac{3}{4}$ x $3\frac{3}{8}$ x $43\frac{1}{2}$	[19.1 x 85.7 x 1104.9]	42 [1066.8] between tenons
2	vertical trim @ drawers	$\frac{3}{4}$ x $\frac{7}{8}$ x $3\frac{3}{8}$	[19.1 x 22.2 x 85.7]	
1	vertical trim @ drawers	$\frac{3}{4}$ x $2\frac{1}{2}$ x $3\frac{3}{8}$	[19.1 x 63.5 x 85.7]	
4	drawer stretchers	$\frac{3}{4}$ x $3\frac{3}{8}$ x $27\frac{1}{2}$	[19.1 x 85.7 x 698.5]	
2	drawer fronts	$\frac{3}{4}$ x $3\frac{3}{8}$ x $18\frac{7}{8}$	[19.1 x 85.7 x 479.4]	opening
8	corbels	$\frac{3}{4}$ x $2\frac{3}{4}$ x $14\frac{1}{2}$	[19.1 x 69.9 x 368.3]	

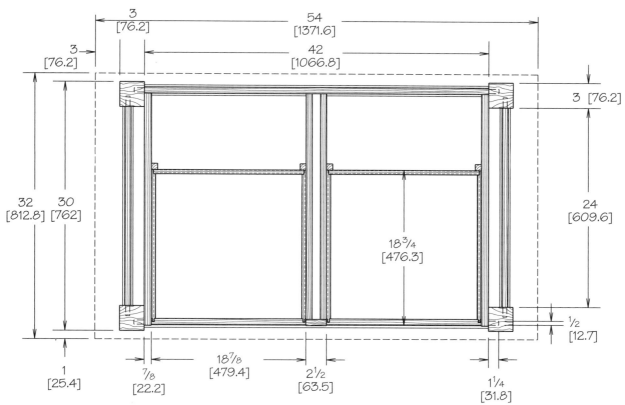

3
[76.2]

3
[76.2]

54
[1371.6]

42
[1066.8]

3 [76.2]

24
[609.6]

32
[812.8]

30
[762]

18³/₄
[476.3]

¹/₂
[12.7]

1
[25.4]

⁷/₈
[22.2]

18⁷/₈
[479.4]

2¹/₂
[63.5]

1¹/₄
[31.8]

Plan through drawers

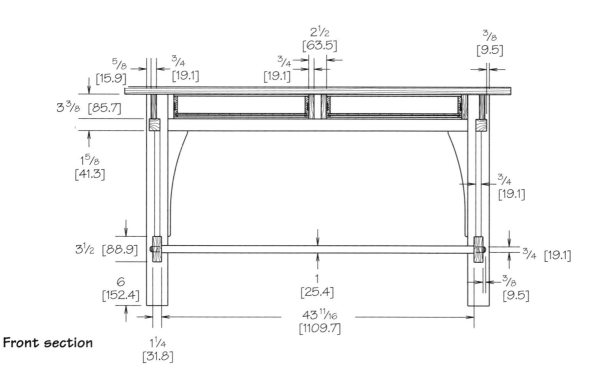

2¹/₂
[63.5]

³/₈
[9.5]

⁵/₈
[15.9]

³/₄
[19.1]

³/₄
[19.1]

3³/₈ [85.7]

1⁵/₈
[41.3]

³/₄
[19.1]

3¹/₂ [88.9]

³/₄ [19.1]

6
[152.4]

1
[25.4]

³/₈
[9.5]

43¹¹/₁₆
[1109.7]

Front section

1¹/₄
[31.8]

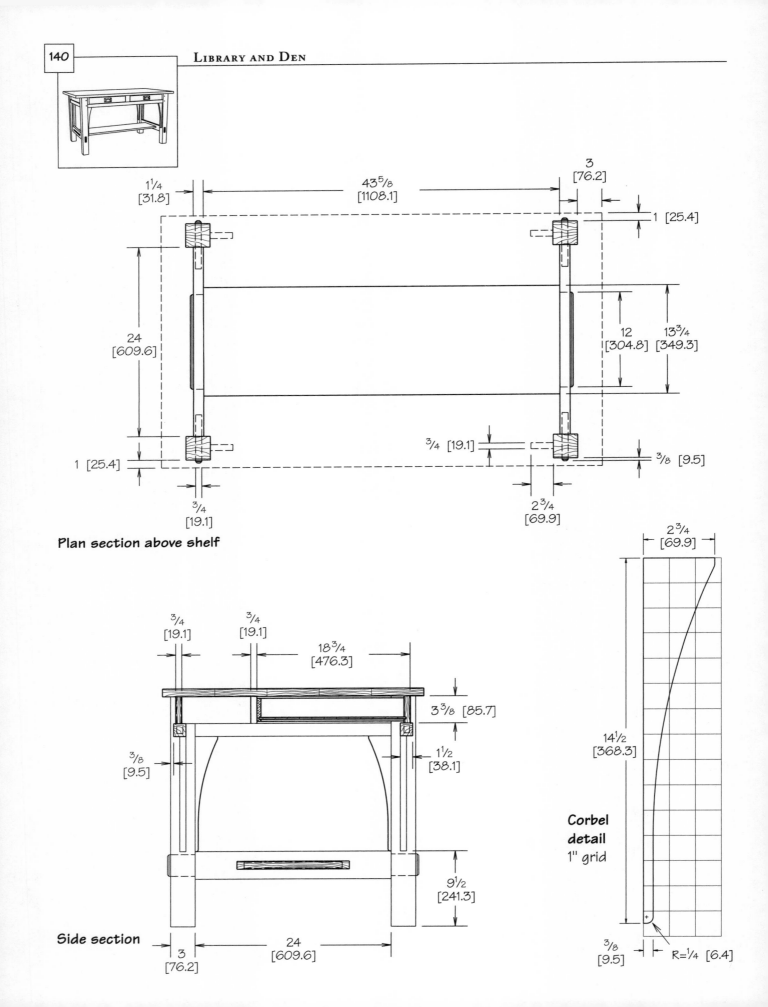

1¼ [31.8]

43⅝ [1108.1]

3 [76.2]

1 [25.4]

24 [609.6]

12 [304.8]

13¾ [349.3]

¾ [19.1]

1 [25.4]

⅜ [9.5]

¾ [19.1]

2¾ [69.9]

Plan section above shelf

¾ [19.1]

¾ [19.1]

18¾ [476.3]

3⅜ [85.7]

⅜ [9.5]

1½ [38.1]

9½ [241.3]

Side section

3 [76.2]

24 [609.6]

2¾ [69.9]

14½ [368.3]

Corbel detail 1" grid

⅜ [9.5]

R=¼ [6.4]

CHARLES LIMBERT LAMP TABLE

19 x 19 x 29 [483 x 483 x 737]

Mitering the four sides together can be intimidating. The angles work out to barely more than 45° for the miter, and a little more than 2° for the taper at the saw. Practice on some scrap to get the settings right. When putting the whole thing together, assemble two sets of the sides, and then the shelf, before gluing on the last two sides.

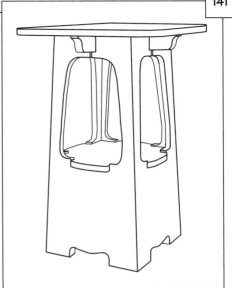

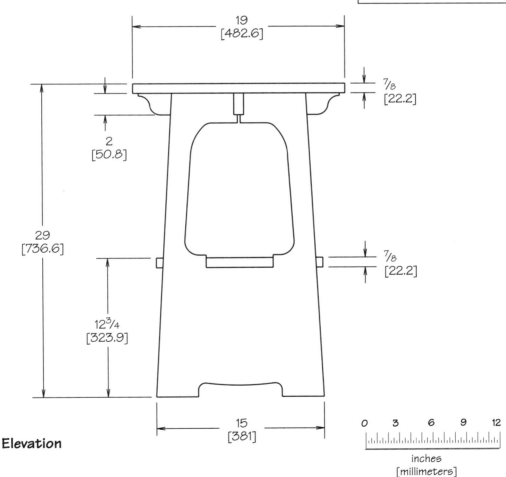

19
[482.6]

7/8
[22.2]

2
[50.8]

29
[736.6]

7/8
[22.2]

12 3/4
[323.9]

15
[381]

Elevation

0 3 6 9 12

inches
[millimeters]

Charles Limbert Lamp Table

QTY	PART	SIZE		NOTES
4	sides	³⁄₄ x 15 x 28 ³⁄₁₆	[19.1 x 381 x 712]	3 degree angle on ends
1	shelf	⁷⁄₈ x 14⁷⁄₈ x 14⁷⁄₈	[22.2 x 377.8 x 377.8]	
1	top	⁷⁄₈ x 19 x 19	[22.2 x 482.6 x 482.6]	
4	corbels	⁷⁄₈ x 2 x 4	[22.2 x 50.8 x 101.6]	

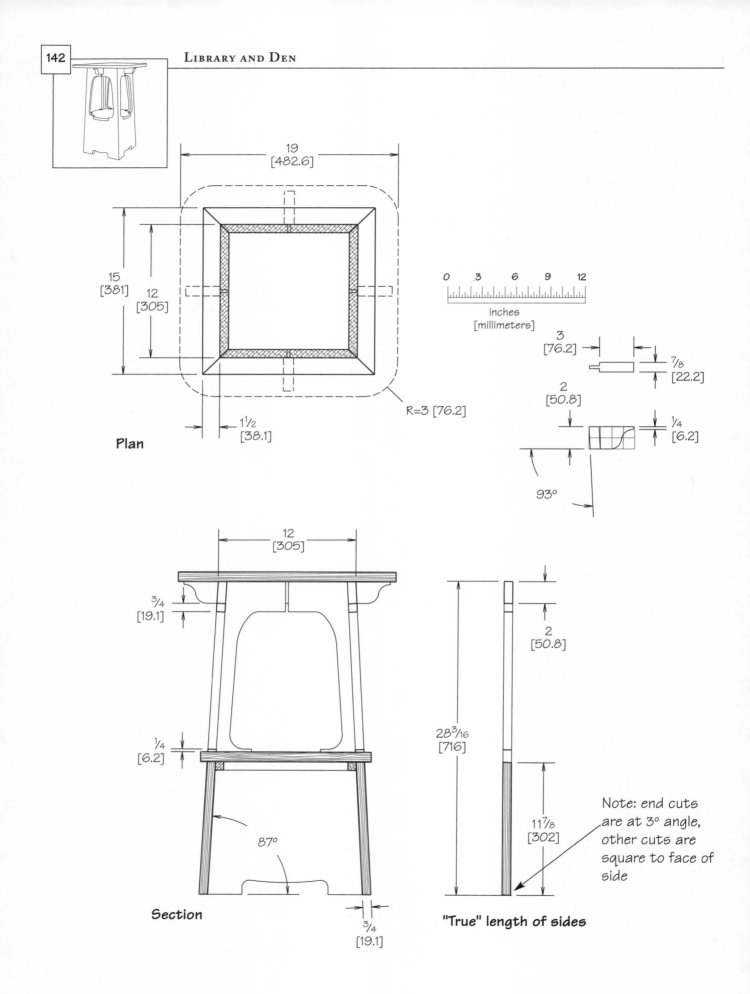

19
[482.6]

15
[381]

12
[305]

1½
[38.1]

R=3 [76.2]

Plan

0   3   6   9   12
inches
[millimeters]

3
[76.2]

⅞
[22.2]

2
[50.8]

¼
[6.2]

93°

12
[305]

¾
[19.1]

¼
[6.2]

87°

Section

¾
[19.1]

28³⁄₁₆
[716]

2
[50.8]

11⅞
[302]

Note: end cuts
are at 3° angle,
other cuts are
square to face of
side

"True" length of sides

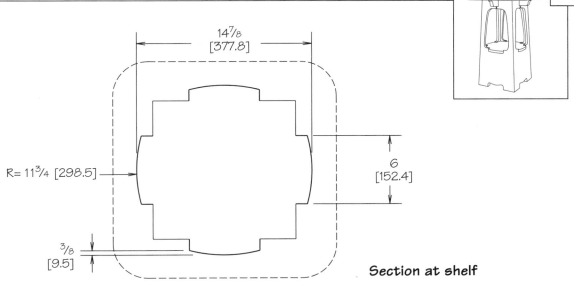

14⁷/₈
[377.8]

6
[152.4]

R= 11³/₄ [298.5]

³/₈
[9.5]

Section at shelf

4⁷/₁₆
[112.7]

1³/₈
[34.9]

³/₈ [9.5]

⁷/₈
[22.2]

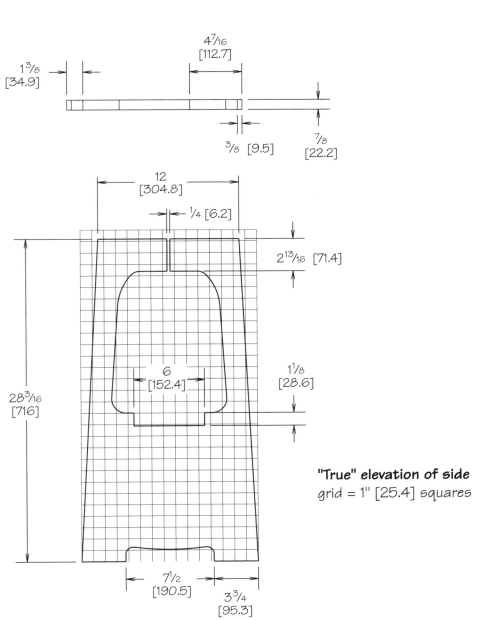

12
[304.8]

¹/₄ [6.2]

2¹³/₁₆ [71.4]

6
[152.4]

1¹/₈
[28.6]

28³/₁₆
[716]

"True" elevation of side
grid = 1" [25.4] squares

7¹/₂
[190.5]

3³/₄
[95.3]

INDEX

LARGE-FORMAT PRINTS

Large-format prints of the project plans in this book are also available. These prints are plotted directly from AutoCAD, with color enhancements. Each set of prints includes regular orthographic views, details, and sections, plus a bill of materials. For ordering information and prices, please contact Cambium Press, 203-778-5610, or on the Internet at www.CAMBIUMPRESS.com, or go to the author's website, www.CRAFTSMANPLANS.com.